Choices at the End of Life

Choices at the End of Life

Finding Out What Your Parents Want
before It's Too Late

Linda Norlander, RN, MS,
and Kerstin McSteen, RN, MS

Fairview Press
Minneapolis

Published by Fairview Press, a division of Fairview Health Services, 2450 Riverside Avenue, Minneapolis, Minnesota 55454.

Library of Congress Cataloging-in-Publication Data

Norlander, Linda, 1949-
    Choices at the end of life : finding out what your parents want before it's too late / Linda Norlander, Kerstin McSteen.
       p. cm.
    Includes bibliographical references and index.
    ISBN 1-57749-103-3 (pbk. : alk. paper)
       1. Aging parents—Care—Decision making. 2. Terminal care—Decision making. 3. Adult children of aging parents—Family relationships. I. McSteen Kerstin, 1959- II. Title.

    R726.8 .N67 2001
    362.1'75—dc21   2001033030

First Printing: October 2001
Printed in the United States of America
04 03 02 01   6 5 4 3 2 1

Cover: *Cover design by Laurie Ingram Duren*
Interior: Dorie McClelland, Spring Type and Design

Language from the Minnesota Health Care Directive (page 102) used with permission.

Ethical will (page 72) taken from http://www.ethicalwill.com. Used with permission.

Medical Disclaimer:
This publication is designed to provide accurate and authoritative information in regard to the subject matter covered. It is sold with the understanding that the publisher is not engaged in the provision or practice of medical, nursing, or professional healthcare advice or services in any jurisdiction. If medical advice or other professional assistance is required, the services of a qualified and competent professional should be sought. Fairview Press is not responsible or liable, directly or indirectly, for any form of damages whatsoever resulting from the use (or misuse) of information contained in or implied by these documents.

For a free current catalog of Fairview Press titles, please call toll-free 1-800-544-8207. Or visit our Web site at www.fairviewpress.org.

ACKNOWLEDGMENTS

We want to acknowledge the Allina Foundation for its commitment to improving care at the end of life, and the Anderson Center for Interdisciplinary Studies for its commitment to writers and other artists.

We thank our colleagues for their support and inspiration: Barry Baines, MD; Edward Ratner, MD; Judy Young; and Brenda Paul.

A very special thanks to our manuscript readers for their time, patience, and honesty: Rusty Holman, MD; Sue Johnson; Marcia Kelly; Jane O'Brien; Judy Young; and our ever-suffering spouses, Tom McSteen and Jerome Norlander.

We thank our families for putting up with us while we wrote the book; Jerome Norlander, who read, edited, and listened; Bree Norlander, who commented and edited; and Tom McSteen, who believed this was a book worth writing.

In memory of
Wally and Vera Norlander,
who had the courage to sit at the kitchen table,
talk about their wishes,
and write their wishes down.

CONTENTS

I'm not afraid to die, I just don't want to be there when it happens.
Woody Allen

Elinor and Her Daughters

As a hospice nurse in the early 1990s, Maureen was asked to talk with two daughters about hospice care for their elderly mother. Elinor had suffered a nearly fatal stroke and was in a coma. The daughters had been offered two options: hospice care to keep Elinor comfortable until she died, or a feeding tube that might prolong her life.

Maureen suspected that Elinor would not recover and that a feeding tube would only prolong her dying. For the two daughters, however, this was a complex decision of life and death. One daughter was in favor of hospice care and letting nature take its course. She felt that a feeding tube would be torture for her mother. The other daughter felt strongly about inserting the feeding tube. In her mind, the feeding tube was the difference between life and death. Not putting it in would make her responsible for her mother's death.

Maureen watched the tension mount as the two daughters discussed the options. Their distress grew as they struggled to come to a decision. Finally, Maureen said, "It's clear you're having a hard time coming to an agreement. Why don't we consider what your mother would have wanted and abide by her wishes. Did you ever discuss her care wishes with her?"

They stopped arguing and looked at her. "Yes."

"And what did she say?"

"She said, 'When the time comes, I know you'll make the right decision.'"

It's a scene that's played out across the country, day after day. We think we will know what to do in a medical crisis, but when the time comes, we realize that we have no idea what our loved ones would want. To further complicate the matter, family members can be irrevocably split over how a loved one should be cared for.

Once called "baby boomers," those of us born between 1946 and 1964 are now "aging boomers." And while we're aging, our parents are aging, too. In fact, many of us are sandwiched between the needs of our growing children and elderly parents. As one tired boomer recently said, "I'm not in the 'sandwich generation,' I'm in the 'club-sandwich generation.' My children, my parents, and my grandparents all need me."

With our parents joining the ranks of the elderly, and sometimes the frail elderly, we are increasingly drawn into the arena of health and healthcare decisions. This is new territory for boomers, and for society in general. In 1900, the average life expectancy was forty-seven years. Most people died suddenly and quickly, usually as the result of an infection or accident. Today, the average life expectancy is seventy-eight, and rising.

With the advent of amazing medical innovations, many of the old causes of death have been eliminated, or at least postponed. People now recover from heart attacks and go on to live for years with new cardiac drugs, pacemakers, and other marvels of technology. Kidney failure can be treated with transplants or dialysis. Cancer can be cured or forced into remission. We now live longer, and in better health.

Since the introduction of penicillin in 1940, the rapid progress of medical knowledge and technology has been staggering. But this progress has created a new generation of aging people who often suffer from chronic disease. And despite all our medical advances, we have not yet discovered a cure for death. Our lifetime mortality rate remains at 100 percent.

As our parents and loved ones age, they will face an array of medical decisions and choices that our ancestors would never have imagined. Helping our parents sort out what makes sense for them, and what does not, might be one of the most important gifts we can give to them.

A Kitchen Table Discussion

We've written this book for baby boomers who want to be better prepared to talk with their parents about the inevitable. A discussion at the kitchen table, perhaps over a cup of coffee, can be the key to honoring our parents' wishes. It can also be a tremendous help in wading through difficult choices in the future.

Choices at the End of Life is designed to help prevent the warfare that may have put a lifelong wedge between Elinor's two daughters. It is a commonsense guide to fostering a discussion with parents and loved ones about healthcare planning, advance directives, and other sticky issues that we inevitably face as our parents age.

Of course, every family is different. We come from divorced families, stepfamilies, and estranged families. We are products of mixed and varying cultures. We are children of the rich, of the poor, and of everything in between.

In fact, many of us are faced with advance care planning for loved ones other than our parents—aunts, uncles, grandparents, cousins, and even good friends. The guidelines and suggestions offered here may be adapted for each of these situations. Though the specifics may differ, the principles remain the same.

A note to parents of baby boomers: *Choices at the End of Life* translates across the generations. If you are a parent with adult children who don't want to talk about your wishes for medical care, you can still use the guidelines in this book.

What Is a Kitchen Table Discussion?

In this book, the phrase "kitchen table discussion" refers to a thoughtful family conversation about healthcare wishes and goals at the end of life. Because the kitchen table is frequently where family discussions are held and decisions are made, it is often the most comfortable place for this conversation. We refer to the content of the discussion as "advance care planning" because it is meant to pave the way for decisions that might have to be made as a loved one's health changes.

Of course, a kitchen table discussion does not have to take place at the kitchen table. For many people, the living-room coffee table may be suitable; for others, Aunt Susie's porch may suffice; and for some, the nursing home lounge may be necessary. It's not the setting that's important, it's the comfort level.

The goal of a kitchen table discussion is three-fold:

- to understand what kind of care your parents and loved ones would want at the end of their lives,
- to determine who will speak for them in health-related matters if ever they cannot speak for themselves, and
- to put these wishes in written form (in a living will or healthcare directive).

The benefits of having a kitchen table discussion are many:

- avoiding unwanted medical treatment;
- resolving disagreements about particular medical treatments before a crisis occurs;
- bringing worries and anxieties into the open; and
- strengthening relationships.

Above all, this courageous conversation is a gift that you and your parents can give to one another.

A kitchen table discussion is more than getting together and filling out a piece of paper (the advance directive). The value in talking with your parents lies in coming together as a family and understanding how Mom and Dad view their health, goals, and options. This is not a discussion that takes place in one sitting—it is a process, a series of conversations that will occur over time.

Kitchen Table Manners

Though the kitchen table is an informal and comfortable setting, certain rules apply—keep your elbows off the table, eat with your mouth closed, clear your dishes when you're finished. Just as good manners make for an enjoyable dining experience, a few rules will set the stage for a comfortable kitchen table discussion.

- Remember, this is a discussion about your parents' choices, not yours. Whether you agree with them or not, you need to respect your parents' wishes.
- A kitchen table discussion is an ongoing process. Wishes and goals can change over time. Be flexible. What is decided today might not be appropriate a year—or even a month—from now.

- **Above all, keep your sense of humor.** Discussing issues related to death and dying can be deadly (forgive the pun). As Karl Barth said, "Laughter is the closest thing to the grace of God."

How Do I Begin?

Many people feel uncomfortable talking about the inevitability of death. One concerned daughter put it like this: "Mom is eighty-five years old, lives in her own home, drives everywhere, and still grows a huge garden. I know I should talk with her about this, but I can't just sit down with her and say, 'Hey, Mom, you're going to die someday. Can we talk about it?'"

In the following chapters, we will take you through a kitchen table discussion, beginning with when and how to start the conversation. Then, we will discuss some of the medical choices you might face. For example, what does it mean if the doctor says, "Your father can no longer swallow—it's time to consider a feeding tube" or "We have a choice now between life support and comfort care"? We will also identify resources that can help you and your parents make important decisions.

Perhaps most important, we will provide tips on how to talk about the things that matter most to your parents. What do they value? Who is important to them? What do they want their lives to be like as they approach the final stretch of the road? If you understand the answers to these questions, you will better understand the choices they make about their healthcare.

And let us not forget the legal paperwork. An effective kitchen table discussion involves filling out legal documents pertaining to healthcare decisions. In chapter 8 we will discuss important paperwork that not only outlines medical treatment preferences, but also names an individual who can speak for your parents if they are unable to speak for themselves. The legal documents have different names, depending on the state in which you live. Documents dealing with treatment choices are called "advance directives," "living wills," or "healthcare directives." They are all essentially the same thing. The person who is given the power to speak for your parents is called a "healthcare proxy," "healthcare representative," "healthcare agent," or "durable medical power of attorney."

Wally and His Family

About the time that Elinor's daughters were struggling with the feeding tube decision, Wally was eager to talk about his healthcare wishes. He had just finished a course of radiation for throat cancer and wanted to fill out a living will.

"Write it out so they won't do anything special to keep me alive," he said. "I just want to be comfortable."

Over the years, Wally had talked with his children and told them all the same thing, "I've lived a good life and I'm not afraid to die. I don't want any of those young doctors doing anything to keep me alive."

Late in the summer of 1999, the time came to test those convictions. Wally was admitted to the hospital for minor surgery. During the hospitalization he lost his ability to swallow. When the doctor suggested a feeding tube, Wally and his family were prepared. Wally told the doctor, "If you're giving me the choice between the slow route with this feeding thing or the fast route, I want the fast one." His wife, children, and grandchildren backed him up—they knew he did not want the feeding tube. Wally was able to refuse the tube on his own. Had he been unable to do so, his family would have refused it for him. They knew his wishes.

Wally died the way he wanted to die—in peace and surrounded by his family. We dedicate this book to Wally, his family, and all who are facing decisions about end-of-life care.

1

Planning a Kitchen Table Discussion

Aging seems to be the only available way to live a long life.
Daniel Francois Esprit Auber

If you were to sit down with your father and bravely ask, "Dad, where would you like to die?" he would likely respond, "At home." According to a recent Gallup poll, 88 percent of adults would prefer to die in their own home or a family member's home.[1] In reality, however, most people in the United States die in hospitals or nursing homes.

If you were to then ask your father, "Dad, have you talked with anyone about this or written it down?" he would likely say, "No." A 1999 survey shows that nearly half of all Americans say they will rely on family and friends to carry out their wishes at the end of life; yet,

75 percent of these Americans have not made their wishes known or put anything in writing. While that may not seem unusual or alarming, consider this: More than 70 percent of people who die in the United States each year are faced with tough decisions about the kind of care they will receive.[2]

When people do not receive the end-of-life care that they want, it is often due to lack of preparation. Many decisions are left to the very end, when it may be too late to honor a person's wish to be at home, or to be made comfortable, or to have the family at his or her bedside. As Linda Emanuel, MD, vice president of ethics for the American Medical Association, says, "We have an entire healthcare system not friendly to end-of-life care, a workforce not educated to end-of-life care, and an entire population just climbing out of the era when it was taboo to talk about dying."[3] As a result, too many people end up dying in non-family-friendly settings. Consider Richard's story:

My father had very bad lung problems. The last time he had trouble breathing, he was taken to the emergency room. They put him on a respirator and shipped him to the intensive care unit. With all the machinery and activity, the noise was awful. Dad couldn't speak because of the tube down his throat. They'd only let us in to see him for a few minutes every hour. The doctors never talked with us about the possibility that he would die. My last memory of Dad was a look of helplessness in his eyes when I told him, "Everything will be all right." He died alone. I never had a chance to say goodbye.

It doesn't have to be that way.

When to Have the Discussion

Like any gathering, formal or informal, a kitchen table discussion involves preparation. Several things need to be decided ahead of time. The first question to ask is, "When should we start talking with Mom and Dad about health decisions?" Ideally, the answer is simple: "Right now." In reality, however, procrastination will rear its ugly head, especially if Mom and Dad are healthy. The more important question is, "When is it crucial that we start talking?" The answer to that is more complex: When you have an elephant in the living room.

The Elephant in the Living Room

Years ago, modern pioneers in chemical dependency treatment coined the phrase "the elephant in the living room" to describe our tendency to ignore a loved one's drinking problem. Everyone knows the problem is there, but no one dares talk about it.

In the arena of healthcare decisions, the elephant in the living room is the unspoken mixture of fears and worries we have when a parent's health changes. For example, Mom might be quite ill, perhaps in the process of receiving treatment meant to cure her, to prolong her life, or to make her comfortable. Perhaps she is showing obvious signs of decline, such as weakness, lack of appetite, and weight loss. Everyone can see the changes occurring, but no one wants to be the one to bring it up. After all, this is scary stuff. Talking about it will make it real.

Instead, the family takes part in a "conspiracy of kindness," ignoring and avoiding this scary and uncomfortable topic. The elephant's presence is unmistakable; yet, everyone hopes they will wake up one morning and the elephant will have disappeared, like a bad dream.

Unfortunately, the elephant doesn't go away. Instead, it grows larger, becomes smellier and more problematic, and takes up more space in peoples' lives. Having to constantly step around the elephant begins to wear on everyone in the family, including Mom.

It often takes a crisis before family members are willing to acknowledge the elephant, but by then it has usually done some serious damage.

Several circumstances should trigger the question, "Do we have an elephant here?":

- a change in health;
- a health scare or crisis; or
- a serious diagnosis, such as cancer, diabetes, or
  lung disease.

A Change in Health

Have you noticed subtle, or maybe not-so-subtle, changes in your parents' health or behavior? Warning signs include:

- weight loss;
- difficulty with everyday tasks, such as bathing or getting to
  the bathroom;
- difficulty with cleaning, preparing meals, monitoring medications, or paying bills;
- increased confusion or forgetfulness;
- an increase in the number of falls and other accidents,
  which may or may not result in injury; and
- concerned calls from neighbors.

Sometimes it is difficult to notice changes as they occur, especially when you see your parents on a regular basis. Subtle changes are often overlooked or dismissed as Mom or Dad "having a bad day." Often it is the out-of-town relative or friend who is able to clearly see the situation.

Jane, a home care nurse, relates this story:

I had just started working with Mrs. Kutchinski, an elderly woman who had recently been hospitalized for heart problems. She had a daughter, Nancy, and a son, Stephen, both of whom lived out of state and visited only once or twice a year. Another daughter, Helen, lived right next door and saw her mother several times a day. Nancy and Stephen returned home to see their mother after her hospital stay. They were shocked at the changes they observed since last they had seen her eight or nine months ago. During my second visit to Mrs. Kutchinski's home, all three siblings were present and the room was quietly tense.

After I had completed my assessment, Mrs. Kutchinski went to take a nap. I spent the next hour listening to Nancy and Stephen describe the changes they saw in their mother, including weight loss, weakness, and poor balance. The last time they had seen her, their mother had been raking leaves and preparing the turkey for Thanksgiving dinner.

At first, Helen felt hurt and defensive about these observations, as if she were being held personally responsible for her mother's decline. But as the three siblings talked more about what had gone on since their last visit, Helen began to realize how much of her life was spent helping her mother. Her mother's health had declined so gradually that she had barely registered the change.

Although Mrs. Kutchinski was mentally clear and managed her own finances and correspondence, Helen did most of her cooking, laundry, grocery shopping, errands, cleaning, and yard work. It took the perspective of time and distance on the part of her siblings for Helen to see how drastically her mother had declined.

Infrequent visitors can bring an invaluable perspective to a cloudy situation. Of course, in the interest of avoiding the elephant, they may not offer their thoughts and observations. You may need to give them permission: "It's been a while now since you've seen Mom. How do you think she is doing?" Your concerns may be validated, and you may even be able to enlist the visitor's assistance in approaching your parents on the subject of advance care planning.

If you don't have the advantage of an outside observer and are wondering if you have missed physical or mental changes in your parents, take out the photo album and look at pictures from the last family celebration. Think back to how Mom or Dad was doing at cousin Lisa's birthday or last year's family reunion. Have things changed?

A Health Scare or Crisis

Although the ideal time to talk about care planning is before a crisis, in reality it often takes a scare to prompt a kitchen table discussion. A scare can be any health- or safety-related incident that does not end in disability or death, but does start you thinking about the potential problems that lie ahead.

Jane, the home care nurse, tells of an elderly gentleman dealing with a scare:

I was working with Mr. Woods, who fell in the bathroom one night and lay on the floor for a day and a half before his son found him. Mr. Woods was lucky. He had suffered a concussion and a nasty cut on his head, and was severely dehydrated, but he recovered and returned home after a short hospital stay. When I tried to bring up the subject of planning for the future, Mr. Woods briskly informed me, "I don't plan to fall again!" I doubted that he had planned to fall and lie on the floor for two days in the first place, but the message was very clear: "I am afraid to talk about this, and I won't!" His son stood by, frustrated and helpless. I later came to understand that Mr. Woods' greatest fear was to lose his independence.

Like Mr. Woods, many people associate advance care planning with a loss of independence; however, one of the goals of a kitchen table discussion is to protect you parents' independence. Consider a report issued in March 2000 by the Centers for Disease Control. The CDC found that every year about one-third of older Americans suffer falls that require hospitalization. In fact, the incidence of hip fractures among women sixty-five and older has increased 40 percent between 1988 and 1996, and half of those who break a hip are not able to return to their former level of mobility or independence.[4]

It's true: A simple accident can lead to permanent disability and a loss of independence. That's why it's so important to confront— and find ways to prevent—this terrifying prospect. If your parents have suffered a fall or other health scare, it's time for a kitchen table discussion. Together, you can consider home improvements or equipment—such as bath rails, improved lighting, or a walker— that will reduce your parents' chance of injury and help them maintain their independence.

If a scare isn't enough to prompt a kitchen table discussion, consider a full-blown crisis. Imagine: One of your parents is in the hospital emergency room or intensive care unit. Perhaps Dad has been in a car accident, or Mom has had a stroke. As the physician explains the condition and options for treatment, he or she is looking to you for guidance. Should they keep your parent on life support? What about treatments that will keep the heart beating, but won't guarantee that your parent will ever be able to go back home again? In the middle of an emotional crisis, you are being asked to make decisions that could literally mean the death of someone you love. Would you know what Mom or Dad would want?

By the time your parents are admitted to the hospital, it may be too late to ask. Think back to the story of Elinor and her daughters on page 1. The sisters had their mother's best interests at heart, but they had interpreted those interests according to their own beliefs and values. Who knows what Elinor would have wanted?

In another example, Al, a widower, was in his mid-eighties when he suffered his second heart attack. As soon as he was well enough to return home, his children said, "We've been through this twice now, Dad. We are not going to do it again without knowing what you want." And there, in his kitchen, they talked. Today, Al reports, "It helps me that they are clear now about what I want, and it certainly helps them."

A Serious Diagnosis

The diagnosis of a life-threatening or life-limiting illness can be a powerful motivation for advance care planning. Imagine that your elderly mother, who has never been sick with anything more than a cold, is suddenly diagnosed with cancer. Cancer is usually serious enough to warrant an open conversation about life goals, values, and long-term care preferences. But cancer is not the only disease that should stimulate such a discussion. For instance, chronic or congestive heart failure (CHF) is an extremely common condition in the elderly. CHF cannot be cured, and it inevitably gets worse over time. In fact, some cardiologists refer to the latter stages of CHF as "heart cancer." Clearly, a person diagnosed with CHF or another heart ailment should know what to expect as the disease progresses and how the disease will be managed medically.

Other diagnoses that signal the need for a kitchen table discussion include:

- diabetes;
- hip fracture;
- kidney (renal) failure;
- liver disease;
- chronic emphysema (chronic obstructive pulmonary disease, or COPD);

- stroke (cerebrovascular accident, or CVA) or ministroke (transient ischemic attack, or TIA);
- Parkinson's disease;
- Alzheimer's disease;
- ALS (amyotrophic lateral sclerosis, or Lou Gehrig's disease); and
- AIDS.

While terminal illness brings an enormous amount of fear, grief, and stress, it also gives loved ones an opportunity to grow closer to one another at the end of life. Too often we pass this opportunity by, focusing our energies entirely on finding a cure or prolonging life. This focus is often appropriate, but it can prevent us from dealing with the inescapable reality that some illnesses will end life.

Dr. Joanne Lynn, who has done extensive work and research in end-of-life care, has observed: "If we structure the course of fatal illness to have a long pursuit of cure, followed by a short period of dying, we fail to seek out the full possibilities for worthy living throughout the course."[5]

The popular book *Tuesdays with Morrie* tells the story of one man's experience with amyotrophic lateral sclerosis (ALS), a progressive fatal neurological disease. Millions of people have been inspired by Morrie's insights and his willingness to talk about his life, illness, and impending death. As Morrie so aptly points out, "Everyone knows they're going to die, but nobody believes it. . . . There's a better approach. To know you're going to die, and to be prepared for it at any time. That's better. That way you can actually be more involved in your life while you're living."[6]

In other words, now is the time to check for the elephant in the living room.

Getting Motivated

The elephant is taking over. You realize that it's time to sit down at the kitchen table, but something always stops you. As one woman said, "I know I need to talk with Mom and Dad, but I keep making excuses. I guess I just don't know where to start."

Is something keeping you from the table? This section offers several detours around the roadblocks you may encounter.

Fear

Fear is likely your biggest obstacle. Coming to the kitchen table isn't easy if your stomach is queasy, particularly if you're about to confront an elephant. Too often, fear holds us back and prevents us from doing what we know to be the right and good thing. Confront your fears before you confront the elephant, and the elephant may not seem so scary. Consider some of the following fears and see if they ring true for you.

Fear of Being Misinterpreted

Your intentions are honorable. You simply want to get people in your family talking so that if something should happen to your parents, everyone will know what they want. But will your intentions be misconstrued? Will others think your actions are motivated, for example, by the inheritance?

When a friend recently broached the topic of long-term care insurance with her father, his immediate response was, "Long-term care insurance is a benefit only to the heirs of the estate." Taken aback by his statement, she was embarrassed and a little hurt by the implication that this was her reason for bringing it up.

Another friend, a nurse, approached his relatively healthy but aging in-laws with blank copies of a healthcare directive. He explained that he wanted to help them fill out an advance directive so that the kids would know what their wishes would be if they were unable to speak for themselves. With tears in her eyes, his mother-in-law asked, "Am I dying?" Our friend replied, "No. This is so we will know what you want if ever you can't speak for yourself. I filled one out for my own family." His mother-in-law felt better after that.

It's sometimes helpful to compare advance directives with life insurance. As one daughter explained to her father, "Remember when you bought that life insurance policy? You didn't buy it because you were dying, you bought it to protect us. This is simply a different kind of protection."

Fear of Taking Away Hope

Taking away hope is a common fear, especially when the person in question has a fatal or potentially fatal condition. Some people worry that discussing end-of-life issues will convey a sense of resignation, as if everybody has "thrown in the towel," leaving parents or loved ones depressed and without the will to live.

On the contrary, research has shown that discussing end-of-life treatments and preferences can be an overwhelmingly positive experience.[7] When asked how they felt when they thought or talked about advance care planning:

- 71 percent of research participants felt a sense of control;
- 53 percent felt relieved; and
- 53 percent felt cared for.

Some participants also expressed negative emotions:

- 22 percent felt nervous;
- 16 percent felt sad; and
- 6 percent felt that they were giving up.

Interestingly, whether the participants had positive or negative feelings, most still wanted to discuss end-of-life care.

After reviewing 120 studies on advance care planning, researchers discovered that the positive effects of such discussions far outweighed the negative, even when the negative effects included fear of worsening health and fear of abandonment.[8] For example:

- People felt less depressed.
- People felt like others cared about them.
- People felt more in control.
- People were able to integrate dying into the context of a personal history and a good life.
- People felt more certain about their particular treatment preferences, and their choices focused more on comfort.

Fear That Talking about Death Will Make It Happen

Words are powerful, to be sure. Intellectually, we recognize that words are just words, and that saying something out loud does not make it happen. Yet, when we speak about something that is scary or uncomfortable, we often shudder, waiting for the flash of lightning to strike. We think we will jinx things. We knock on wood for protection and luck.

Many people are particularly superstitious about the words *death* and *dying*. Frederick, a teacher in his late fifties, explains:

I know this is pretty silly, but ever since I was a kid, I've avoided using the word "die." I think it goes back to when I was seven or eight

*and my mother overheard me fighting with my friend Jack. I was so
angry with him I said, "I hope you die." Mom took me aside and told me
it was a bad thing to say. I remember her words, "Freddie, think of how
you would feel if it really happened." We never used the word in our
house. We talked about Grandpa "passing on" and Grandma "leaving
us." When Mom recently learned that she had breast cancer, I couldn't
talk with her about the possibility of dying. I couldn't get the words out.*

It helps to state our fears out loud: "I'm afraid that if I talk to
Mom and Dad about end-of-life care, they will get sick and die. But
talking about it won't make it happen, and not talking about it
won't prevent it from happening."

As one social worker puts it, "I know you are worried that if
you talk about dying, it might happen. I want to assure you that if
you don't talk about dying, it will still happen."

Assumptions

It's easy to avoid a kitchen table discussion by telling yourself,
"Advance care planning isn't my responsibility. Someone else will
bring it up." Or worse, "It doesn't matter, because things always
work out somehow." Don't count on it. If you don't start the conversation, chances are that no one will.

Assuming That Advance Care Planning Is the Doctor's Job

Many people rely on medical caregivers to bring up the topic of
advance care planning. This is such a strongly held belief that, in
1991, the federal government enacted legislation called the Patient
Self-Determination Act. This law requires all hospitals, skilled
nursing facilities, health maintenance organizations (HMOs), home
health agencies, and hospices that receive Medicare or Medicaid
reimbursement to 1) inform patients of their right to accept or

refuse medical care, and 2) advise patients of their right to make an advance directive.

The idea behind the law is good: It supports an individual's right to make choices in personal medical matters. Unfortunately, while hospitals and healthcare agencies may adhere to the letter of the law, they often fall short of the law's intent—to encourage patients and their physicians to discuss healthcare wishes, especially regarding life-sustaining treatments.

Typically, when a patient is admitted to a hospital, he or she faces a laundry list of questions. Somewhere between "Social security number?" and "Do you have any allergies?" is the question, "Do you have a living will or healthcare directive?" If the answer is no, patients may be given an envelope of information about advance care planning—an envelope that usually remains unopened. Some people are not so fortunate to be asked the question at the admissions desk: At a recent lung cancer support group, two people recalled being asked if they had a healthcare directive as they lay on a gurney, about to be wheeled into surgery!

Why isn't advance care planning routinely discussed in a medical setting? Shouldn't physicians be the ones to get patients and families thinking and talking about the future? After all, one would assume that care planning would be a matter of course in a long-standing relationship between patient and physician.

The problem with this assumption is that people don't often have a long-standing relationship with a physician. Not long ago, the whole family might have seen the same "family doctor" for decades. Today we are a mobile society, and when we relocate, we must change healthcare providers. People change providers for other reasons, too, including cost and employer health insurance options. To further complicate matters, some physician organizations and HMOs have such large clinic operations that seeing the same doctor twice is a challenge. What's more, many people see several different specialists, which can severely fragment their care.

In one study, patients were asked why they did not approach the doctor about advance care planning, even though their physical condition warranted such a discussion. Most often, patients said they were waiting for their doctor to broach the topic. The doctors, on the other hand, were waiting for the patients.[9] As a family practice doctor said, "I don't bring it up unless the patient asks me about it."

When it comes time to hold a kitchen table discussion, the degree to which a doctor is involved will largely depend on the relationship between patient, family, and physician. But take note: If you are waiting for the physician or any other member of the healthcare team to get the ball rolling, you may be waiting for some time.

Assuming That Things Will Take Care of Themselves

Most of us put a great deal of trust in our ability to handle the unexpected. However, if a crisis occurs before you have had a kitchen table discussion, rest assured that things will take care of themselves—but not necessarily in the way you and your parents would have wanted.

Medical crises tend to take on a life of their own. Remember, emergency medical professionals are trained to act now, ask questions later. Their job is to sustain life, and so they often begin CPR, mechanical ventilation, and other interventions. Afterward, the family must decide whether treatment should be continued or withdrawn. Family members are asked to make this difficult life-and-death decision when, emotionally, they are least equipped to do so.

Annette, a cancer nurse for more than twenty years, once remarked to her brother about how common it is for dying patients to live out their final days connected to every machine available. She said, "When I look at some of these people, all I can think of is Dad and how he would not want to be treated like this." To her surprise, her brother replied, "Oh, yes he would! Technology is there to be used, and Dad would want it to be used to its fullest extent." After this conversation, they concluded that it was time to talk to their father.

Family members can be at opposite ends of the spectrum when it comes to end-of-life decision making. That's why it is so important to discuss treatment preferences up front, rather than trust that things will work out for the best. Studies show that when family members are asked to indicate which treatment options their loved ones would want, their selections are not much better than random chance when compared to their loved ones' actual preferences.[10]

Now that you have taken stock of your own situation and identified possible barriers you may encounter, the kitchen table is set for a discussion. The next chapter, Who's Who in Advance Care Planning, will guide you in deciding which people to invite.

REFERENCES

1. The Gallup Organization, "Knowledge and Attitudes Related to Hospice Care: A Survey" (Washington, D.C.: National Hospice and Palliative Care Organization, 1996).

2. Survey, April 1999 (Washington, D.C.: National Hospice Foundation, 1999).

3. "At Life's End Many Patients Are Denied Peaceful Passing," *New York Times,* 29 May 2000.

4. "CDC: Hip Fractures among Women over 65 Increasing," Associated Press, 31 March 2000.

5. J. Lynn, "Unexpected Returns: Insights from SUPPORT," in *To Improve Health and Health Care,* eds. S. L. Isaacs and J. R. Knickman (San Francisco: Jossey-Bass, 1997), 178.

6. M. Albom, *Tuesdays with Morrie* (New York: Doubleday, 1997), 81.

7. B. Lo, G. A. McLeod, and G. Saika, "Patient Attitudes to Discussing Life-Sustaining Treatment," *Archives of Internal Medicine* 146 (1986): 1613–15.

8. S. H. Miles, R. Koepp, and E. P. Weber, "Advance End-of-Life Treatment Planning: A Research Review," *Archives of Internal Medicine* 156 (1996): 1062–68.

9. L. L. Emanuel, et al., "Advance Directives for Medical Care: A Case for Greater Use," *New England Journal of Medicine* 324 (1991): 889–95.

10. E. J. Emanuel and L. L. Emanuel, "Proxy Decision Making for Incompetent Patients: An Ethical and Empirical Analysis," *Journal of the American Medical Association* 267 (1992): 2067–71.

2

Who's Who in
Advance Care Planning

No matter how many communes anybody invents,
the family always creeps back.

Margaret Mead

The first step in planning a kitchen table discussion is deciding on the guest list. Remember, one person's illness affects the whole family. For the discussion to be effective, it must involve everyone who will be responsible for—or affected by—the decisions that are made.

When Eric talked with his father about advance care planning, he was pleased that his father had given it some thought. There were complications, however:

My mom died over ten years ago and my dad has since remarried. I like my stepmother, but I don't know her very well. When I talked with my dad one day about healthcare decisions if he was dying, he told me not to worry about it. He'd had a long discussion with my stepmother and she knew exactly what he wanted. I said, "That's good, Dad, but what if for some reason she wasn't there for you? I don't know what you would want." It took him quite by surprise. "I really hadn't thought about that," he said. I'm hoping we can pick up this conversation again, once he's had a chance to think about it more.

As Eric pointed out, no one can predict the future. The more people there are who understand your parents' wishes for end-of-life care, the more likely it is that these wishes will be honored.

It's very important to ask your parents who they would like to invite to this discussion. Be sure to consider people outside of the immediate family, including out-of-town relatives, clergy, friends, neighbors, and so on.

Family

The twenty-first-century family includes more than parents and children. Indeed, the boundaries of family extend to stepparents, stepchildren, grandchildren, brothers, sisters, aunts, uncles, even friends. Whether you find yourself in the midst of a small family or a "village," it's important to invite the key family players who will be involved with your parents' healthcare decisions.

Out-of-Towners

As we discussed earlier, relatives who live far away and visit infrequently can often add a fresh perspective to your kitchen table discussion. On the other hand, out-of-towners can inadvertently sabotage efforts to talk openly about advance care planning, sometimes even questioning the necessity of the discussion. For family members who must deal with the daily hardships of illness or failing health, this interference can be frustrating. However, when out-of-town relatives are left out of the discussion, they may show up after a crisis occurs and demand care that had previously been considered and decided against. So, unless Mom or Dad says no, it's often best to include the out-of-towners in the kitchen table discussion.

In this day of modern technology, speakerphones and conference calls make it possible for everyone to be included. If scheduling or other problems prevent this, make sure everyone is told that the discussion will be held, then make sure everyone knows the outcome. When a parent fills out a healthcare directive, send everyone a copy. Good communication early on will help to avoid misunderstandings and conflicts later.

Clergy or Spiritual Leaders

Many families find it is helpful to have a rabbi, priest, or pastor present during a kitchen table discussion. Clergy can offer support and guidance for spiritual and religious questions that may arise during the conversation. For example, questions about medical treatments may bring up concerns about assisted suicide. It can also lead to spiritual discussions about sin, forgiveness, and the afterlife. Direction from your parents' faith community can be extremely important here. If a spiritual leader is not available for the discussion, you may want to write down questions or concerns for him or her to address later.

Friends and Neighbors

In today's mobile society, many of us live far away from Mom and Dad. Consequently, our parents often develop close, trusting relationships with their friends and neighbors. As an eighty-eight-year-old widower said, "If something happens to me, my neighbor will probably be the first one to know." If that's the case with your parents, it's important to include friends and neighbors in your kitchen table discussion. These people can have a crucial impact on how your parents' wishes are carried out.

Marie, a hospice coordinator, talks about one neighbor's role in a hospice patient's care:

Ed lived in the house he grew up in. His children were scattered across the country and unable to be with him. When he couldn't live alone anymore, his next-door neighbor said, "I know Ed's greatest hope now is to stay in the neighborhood. I want him to come and live with me." She set up a bed in her dining room so he could look out the window at his house. Because this neighbor understood his wishes, Ed was able to die in the neighborhood in which he had lived all his life.

Tony, a hospice social worker, recalls a similar story:

I was visiting Charlie, a patient whose only living relative was an older brother. Wouldn't you know, two weeks after Charlie signed on for hospice care, the brother dropped dead of a sudden heart attack. Who should step forward to look after Charlie but the bartender from the neighborhood tavern down the street. He stopped in every day to make sure Charlie had food and medicine.

Find out who your parents' friends are, and be sure to include them in the discussion.

Legal Representatives

When planning the guest list for a kitchen table discussion, your parents might ask, "Don't we need our lawyer for this?" We want to be clear: You do not need a lawyer to fill out a healthcare directive or to make it legal; however, it's certainly appropriate to get the input of an attorney, if it makes your parents feel more comfortable. Just make sure that everyone understands the financial arrangements if a lawyer is present.

Healthcare Professionals

Some people want to include a doctor in their care planning discussion; others do not. Recent studies indicate that most people view the kitchen table discussion as an opportunity to strengthen relationships, prepare for the end of life, ease the family's emotional burden, and prevent financial hardship for survivors. Throughout the study, patients expressed confidence that their family would represent their values and wishes to the physician and healthcare team.[1]

However, some families find that the input of healthcare professionals can be extremely valuable. When preparing the guest list, consider all the medical personnel involved in the care of your parents: home care nurses, social workers, case managers, and physicians. These professionals can answer specific questions related to the your parents' physical condition, prognosis, and medical options.

If a healthcare professional does not attend your kitchen table discussion, it's a good idea to write down any medical questions that come up so you can ask them at a later date. Choices can be difficult to make without having all the important information.

REFERENCES

1. P. A. Singer, et al, "Reconceptualizing Advance Care Planning from the Patient's Perspective," *Archives of Internal Medicine* 158 (1998): 879–84.

3

Healthcare Options

What I need is a list of specific unknown problems we will encounter.

From a corporate memo

When you sit down for a cup of coffee, you have choices—regular, decaf, black, cream, and sugar. In healthcare, you also have choices. The trick is to sort through them and figure out which ones are appropriate for your situation. Dad can't walk up to a doctor and say, "I've thought about it and decided I'd rather get a new liver than deal with the one I have." Maybe liver transplantation isn't a possibility, but there are other options worth exploring.

When people are unrealistic about their medical condition or treatment options, often it is not because they are in denial, but because they are in the dark. They don't have the information necessary to make informed choices about their healthcare.

This chapter is about understanding treatment choices. We will define and explain common terms and abbreviations that you and your parents will encounter when completing a healthcare directive. Because this section is heavy on details, you may need to put the book down and take a breather now and then to absorb all the information. Or you might use this section as a reference, picking and choosing those treatments that interest you most or that best apply to your family's particular situation.

Your biggest challenge may be interpreting medical terms and jargon. CPR, DNR, DNI, NG tubes, TPN, intubation, transfusion, dialysis—the list goes on and on. (Feel free to check the glossary at the back of this book as necessary.) Medical language is filled with acronyms, numbers, and long, Latin-sounding words and terms. Because these terms are second nature to medical professionals, doctors and nurses often don't realize that what they are trying to communicate is coming across as gibberish.

Consider the story of LaVerne, a home care patient who had procrastinated before completing a healthcare directive. Finally, with a home care social worker's assistance, she held a kitchen table discussion and documented her wishes:

Yes, I put off doing it, but it wasn't because I didn't want to talk about my health. When you have as many things wrong with you as I do, you certainly think about these things. No, the hard part was knowing what all those terms meant. CPR, DNR, this kind of tube, that kind of tube—hell, I didn't know what all that meant. I needed someone who could explain it. I knew what I wanted—I just didn't know how to handle all those words.

When filling out a healthcare directive, it is not necessary to write down your parents' feelings about every possible treatment. What's important is for you and your parents to understand why a particular treatment may be offered and what effect that treatment may have, including the expected benefits versus the potential risks or burdens. "Risk" refers to possible complications, such as infection or the adverse effects of medication. "Burden" has more to do with posttreatment quality-of-life issues, such as permanently reduced lung capacity or a lifelong dependence on medication.

Remember, your parents' treatment preferences will change over time—your sixty-eight-year-old father may feel very differently about these things than your ninety-five-year-old grandmother—so whatever is decided today should be reviewed on a regular basis.

Life-Supporting Treatments

If your mom called to say, "Uncle Harry collapsed at home and is in the hospital on life support," it could mean many things. He could be in the intensive care unit on a machine that helps him breathe. He could be receiving medicines that help his heart beat normally. He could be hooked up to a machine that filters waste from his body.

Life-supporting treatments replace or support a bodily function that is failing. When a person is expected to recover from an illness or injury, such support is necessary until the body can stabilize and function on its own. When a person is not expected to recover, life support can prolong the dying process and add to the level of pain and suffering.

In Uncle Harry's case, it could be that he has a good chance for recovery, and that life-supporting treatment will allow his body to heal. Or, it could mean that the life-support treatments are keeping him alive, but his body will never recover enough to function on its own. A healthcare directive will generally address treatments related to the latter scenario.

CPR (Cardiopulmonary Resuscitation)

CPR refers to treatments used when a person's heart stops beating or the person stops breathing. CPR can include any of the following:

- mouth-to-mouth breathing;
- intubation and mechanical ventilation (placing a tube down the throat and into the windpipe, then using a machine to push air through the tube and into the lungs);
- chest compressions (pressing on the chest to push blood through the heart);
- defibrillation (electric shock and paddles); and
- drugs to stimulate the heart.

Developed in 1960, CPR has become standard practice on any person without a pulse, no matter what the underlying condition. In the case of drowning, choking, electrocution, drug reaction, surgery, or acute heart attack, CPR can be life saving, especially when it is started immediately and the victim is in relatively good health.

When patients are admitted to a hospital, CPR is often explained inadequately. The doctor or nurse may ask, "If your heart stops, do you want it restarted?" It sounds as easy as flipping a light switch: "Heart stopped? We'll just turn it back on." Who would say no to that? The fact is, CPR is not that simple.

Most of us know about CPR from what we've seen on television and in the movies. The survival rate for people receiving CPR on television is upwards of 65 percent—much better than in real life. Even "realistic" shows like *Rescue 911* tend to focus exclusively on those cases where CPR is effective. This is not surprising, given that the scenarios dramatized are the exact situations for which CPR was developed: drownings, gunshot wounds, car accidents, and other acute injuries.[1]

In reality, CPR performed in a hospital setting yields a survival rate between 5 and 15 percent until hospital discharge. In one study, no patients with widespread infection, advanced cancer, or internal bleeding survived CPR, and only 3 percent of patients with kidney failure survived. CPR started outside a hospital setting is even less effective. If it isn't started within four minutes of a person's collapse, lack of oxygen will cause brain damage or brain death.

Physicians and hospitals often feel obligated to perform CPR on any patient whose heart or breathing has stopped. Likewise, families often insist that CPR be attempted, even when it is unlikely to succeed and may be harmful to their loved one.

When a patient "survives" CPR, it means his or her heart has started beating again. However, because the pressure applied to the chest must be great enough to squeeze the heart, many people end up with broken ribs and severe bruises. Brain damage and tissue damage to the hands, arms, legs, and feet may result from the lack of good oxygen circulating throughout the body. A person often vomits during the resuscitation, and the vomit can be inhaled into the lungs, which can cause pneumonia. After resuscitation, the patient will usually be connected to a ventilator and to machines that monitor vital signs. He or she will likely receive antibiotics to fight infections, as well as multiple intravenous (IV) medications to regulate the heart and blood pressure. The patient may have a tube inserted down the nose or into the stomach for feeding, a tube inserted into the bladder to drain urine, and more.

Many physicians and nurses are beginning to question the value and ethics of starting CPR on everyone whose heart has stopped. They recognize that, like any other medical treatment, CPR is not appropriate in every situation.

Mechanical Ventilation

Mechanical ventilation requires a "breathing machine," commonly called a vent, ventilator, or respirator. The machine forces air into the lungs through a breathing tube, which is generally inserted through the mouth or nose into the trachea, or windpipe. If a person is expected to be on a ventilator for a long time, the doctors will usually perform a tracheotomy, or "trach." In this procedure, a small slit is cut into the throat and trachea, allowing a breathing tube to be inserted through the patient's throat.

A ventilator can help support patients through a short-term medical crisis. It may also help people with neurological illnesses or injuries, such as ALS or spinal cord injuries, to survive for years with a good quality of life. For people who are terminally ill though, the ventilator tends to prolong the dying process. It cannot cure or reverse the illness.

Artificial Nutrition and Hydration

Artificial nutrition and hydration refers to a variety of therapies meant to prevent malnutrition or dehydration in patients who cannot swallow. While this topic may seem mild when compared to such invasive procedures as intubation and ventilation, it is perhaps the most emotionally charged issue that families face. Food and water are basic elements of life, but eating and drinking satisfy more than just our physical needs; they are woven into the emotional, social, religious, and cultural fabric of almost every family and community. We show our love and care for others by cooking for them, preparing a favorite dish, sharing a meal, or raising a toast.

Julia, a hospice nurse, tells of her work with an elderly couple:

Oscar was dying from prostate cancer. His wife, Ethel, was efficiently and lovingly attending to his needs as his condition worsened. Every time

I came to visit, Ethel was cooking or baking, and she prided herself on her skills in the kitchen. As Oscar became weaker and was confined to bed, Ethel struggled to get him to eat. I explained that a person's appetite naturally decreases as he or she declines. I encouraged Ethel to let Oscar dictate what and how much he would eat and drink, emphasizing that his body would tell him what it needed. Ethel understood and accepted this, at least initially.

One day I arrived to find Ethel very upset. We sat together on the couch while Ethel sobbed, explaining how hurt she was by Oscar's rejection of her cooking. "I've tried everything," she said. "I've spent hours cooking his favorite meals, only to have him take one or two small bites and push it away." I realized that this was not just an issue of decreasing appetite; Ethel was interpreting Oscar's rejection of food as a rejection of her. Ethel had spent more than fifty years showing her love for Oscar by cooking for him. Now that he wasn't interested in eating, she did not know how to show him that she loved him.

At first glance, keeping someone fed and hydrated appears to be a basic comfort measure. Certainly, if healthy people are deprived of food and water, they will suffer from starvation and dehydration. The bodily processes of a healthy person, however, differ greatly from those of a dying person.

Surprisingly, people who are in the end stages of life rarely complain of hunger or thirst. In fact, studies conducted over the past fifteen years show that nutrition and hydration in the last stages of life neither prolong life nor increase comfort.[2] Forcing nutrition or hydration on a patient in the final stages of a terminal illness can cause discomfort and distress.

Artificial Nutrition

As the body grows weaker, a person can eventually lose the ability to safely chew and swallow food. This can lead to coughing, choking on food or liquid, and sometimes breathing food or liquid into the lungs (aspiration), which can cause pneumonia. At this stage, physicians may recommend, or families might inquire about, a feeding tube.

A nasogastric tube (NG tube) is a flexible tube that is inserted into the stomach through the nose. A gastric tube (G tube) is surgically inserted directly into the stomach. Water, medications, and special nutritional formulas can be administered through either kind of tube.

A feeding tube may help a patient survive a debilitating, but reversible, condition. The decision to place a feeding tube depends largely on individual circumstances. Compare the following scenarios:

Jack, sixty-three years old, had suffered a stroke. Even though the stroke was severe, his physicians were hopeful that he would regain much of his functioning. The stroke had left him unable to swallow, so an NG tube was inserted through his nose. Several weeks after the stroke, Jack recovered much of his ability to swallow. With therapy, he was eventually able to eat and drink on his own, and the tube was removed.

Joan, seventy-one, also had a stroke; however, the extent of damage to her brain was much worse than Jack's. Her doctor did not expect her to regain consciousness or to breathe on her own again. Because the feeding tube could not possibly reverse the damage done by the stroke, Joan's doctor recommended against it. Joan's family agreed. The medical team made sure Joan was comfortable, and she died peacefully a few days later.

Another form of artificial nutrition is called total parenteral nutrition (TPN), or hyperalimentation (hyperal, or HA). This is a highly concentrated and chemically complex formula that provides water and complete nutritional requirements. TPN is administered through a special catheter that is inserted into a large vein.

Depending on the type of catheter, insertion may require a minor surgical procedure. Because the catheter is vulnerable to infection, it requires scrupulous care and monitoring.

TPN can help relatively healthy people get through a severe illness when they're unable to eat. Take the case of Darla, a fifty-year-old woman with breast cancer. During chemotherapy, Darla suffered from nausea and vomiting so severe that she had difficulty keeping anything down. TPN helped meet her nutritional needs until the nausea subsided and she was able to eat again.

Artificial Hydration

For patients who are unable to drink fluids, a needle can be placed in a vein (IV) or under the skin (subcutaneously) to administer simple sugar or saline solutions. This is called artificial hydration. The procedure provides few calories and little, if any, nutrition. Generally, the risks involved with an IV are minimal, but the needle must be changed about every three days or when it malfunctions.

It's important to understand that dehydration (lack of fluids) in the end stages of life is a natural process. Dehydration produces an analgesic (pain-killing) effect that actually helps keep a dying person more comfortable. Hydration can interfere with this natural comfort measure.

Pros and Cons of Artificial Nutrition and Hydration

Artificial nutrition and hydration may help a nonterminal patient survive a serious illness or injury. A feeding tube can provide nutrition until the patient is able to eat on his or her own, and intravenous fluids can sometimes correct a fluid or electrolyte imbalance, which may stabilize the patient and may even reverse symptoms.

When a person is dying, however, artificial nutrition and hydration will not prolong life, and may cause a great deal of discomfort. Inserting a feeding tube can be a painful, invasive procedure, and tube feedings may cause loose stools or diarrhea, which can lead to bedsores. Intravenous fluids can cause an accumulation of fluid in the body, which may lead to increased urine production and a subsequent loss of bladder control; nausea and vomiting; fluid in the lungs that can cause difficulty breathing; edema (swelling) in the hands, feet, and face; ascites (accumulation of fluid in the abdomen); and pain from excess fluid pressure on tissues and organs.

If a person is dying, families should consider two more points before making a decision about artificial nutrition and hydration. First, these treatments require skills and equipment that caregivers must learn to manage at home. This can detract from time spent comforting or simply being with the dying person. Second, religious concerns may influence an individual's choice. Many religious organizations have issued statements supporting the decision to refuse or discontinue artificial nutrition and hydration, declaring it an ethically and morally acceptable alternative. Nevertheless, if you have questions about this matter, it is best to seek guidance from your faith community.

Dialysis

When a person's kidneys stop working, dialysis treatment can replace kidney function. There are two kinds of dialysis: hemodialysis and peritoneal dialysis.

Hemodialysis

Hemodialysis cleans a person's blood using a dialysis machine. During treatment, the patient's blood travels through tubes into the machine, which filters out wastes and extra fluids. The newly cleaned blood then flows through another set of tubes back into the patient's body.

To receive hemodialysis treatment, the individual must undergo a surgical procedure that will create an access to the bloodstream. The access (or shunt) allows blood to be carried from the body to the dialysis machine and then back into the body.

Treatments take from four to six hours and are usually done three times per week at a clinic or hospital. Common complications during dialysis treatments include low blood pressure, nausea, and headaches. Serious complications include clotting problems and infection. People on long-term hemodialysis struggle with quality-of-life issues. They tend to feel sick a lot, take many medications, and feel restricted by the dialysis schedule.

Peritoneal Dialysis

With peritoneal dialysis, a special solution is administered through a tube stitched into the lower abdomen. This solution absorbs bodily wastes that would normally be removed by the kidneys. The solution is then drained from the body. Although less invasive than hemodialysis, this procedure must be done several times per day. Treatments are done at home. The greatest risk is infection.

Antibiotics

Antibiotics are such a routine medical intervention these days, many people consider them a standard treatment, not a life-support measure. In some situations, antibiotics can save a person's life. In the case of terminal illness, however, antibiotics can either ease a person's discomfort or prolong his or her suffering.

When deciding whether to treat an infection with antibiotics, consider the long-term outcome. For example, when a patient is dying, a bladder infection can cause unnecessary pain and distress; it should therefore be treated. Pneumonia, on the other hand, can bring a quick and relatively painless death before more difficult symptoms arise. (For this reason, pneumonia has been called the "Old Man's Friend.") Treating pneumonia may only prolong the person's dying. Consider Lily's situation:

Lily had completed a healthcare directive specifically stating that she did not want antibiotics if it would only prolong her dying. Soon after, she had a massive stroke. Lily was not expected to survive, much less recover. Unaware of the healthcare directive, a physician wrote an order for an antibiotic to treat a developing pneumonia. Lily's nephew, Josh, was the healthcare agent. "It took some discussion with the doctor, but Aunt Lily had been very clear on this point," he says. "We ended up not starting the antibiotic, and she died very comfortably a few days later. I hate to think of her lying there, prolonging the inevitable, just because we are so used to giving people antibiotics when they start to run a fever."

Blood Transfusions

Blood transfusions can be life-saving for people with certain diseases or injuries. If someone is terminally ill, though, a blood transfusion will not reverse the course of the illness. It may help to alleviate symptoms of fatigue and shortness of breath, but rarely in the final stages of a terminal disease.

The patient usually must go to a hospital or clinic for the blood to be administered, and the transfusion may take from four to eight hours (or more, depending on how many units are being transfused). People with certain religious beliefs, such as Jehovah's Witnesses, may have strong feelings about not accepting blood products.

Surgery

In the United States, surgery is often recommended if a condition is likely to respond to it, and if the surgeon feels that the patient can survive the procedure. Indeed, surgery may be the best option in some cases. Too often, though, people don't realize that many conditions, such as bowel obstructions and fractured hips, can be managed without surgery in a way that will ensure comfort, especially when a person is terminally ill.

When confronted with the prospect of surgery, ask the doctor the following questions to determine if surgery is the best option:

- "If Mom survives the surgery, what are her overall prospects for the future?"
- "What are the risks or possible complications of this surgery? Given Dad's current condition, how likely are these to occur?"
- "What are the odds that Mom will return to the same level of functioning as before the surgery?"
- "What would happen if we decided not to do surgery?"
- "Could Dad's condition be managed without surgery?"
- "Is it time to consider hospice care?"

Think about what is important to your parents, and ask specific questions that reflect what they see as an acceptable quality of life. Will Mom be able to work in her garden? Will she be able to get out of bed? Will Dad be able to play cards at the community center every Tuesday? Will he be aware of his surroundings and able to interact with family and friends?

Hospitalization

In the not-so-distant past, terminal patients were likely to spend their final days, weeks, or months in the hospital. Today, the length of the typical hospital stay has decreased significantly, and families are often surprised when the hospital social worker or discharge planner calls to ask, "Which nursing home would you like your father transferred to?"

This is not necessarily a negative development. The role of the hospital is to treat people who are sick or injured and try to make them better. Of course, if a patient is terminally ill, getting better is not a possibility. Nevertheless, if this patient is hospitalized, he or she may undergo unwanted tests, procedures, and interventions, including aggressive life-sustaining treatments. As medical ethicist George Annas said, "If dying patients want to retain some control over their dying process, they must get out of the hospital if they are in, and stay out of the hospital if they are out."[3]

It is a good idea to state preferences about hospitalization in a healthcare directive, and to specify the setting in which your parents would prefer to receive care. (Keep in mind that long-term hospitalization is probably not a viable option.) Many chronically or terminally ill nursing home residents are asking their doctor to write a "Do Not Hospitalize" order in their chart so they won't end up in the hospital.

Not Starting Treatment versus Withdrawing Treatment

There is no legal or moral difference between withdrawing a treatment and not starting it in the first place. Emotionally, some families find it more difficult to stop a treatment once it has been started. It is essential to recognize that stopping or withholding a particular treatment does not cause death; death is caused by the disease or injury.

Nathan had struggled for years with chronic emphysema and heart failure. Nevertheless, he felt strongly that he should be placed on a ventilator if life support became necessary. When in his seventies, Nathan contracted pneumonia and went into the hospital for treatment. There he suffered a heart attack. He was resuscitated and placed on a ventilator, but his condition was very poor and the doctors did not offer much hope that he would ever regain consciousness or be able to breathe on his own. The ventilator was keeping him alive, but it would never cure him or reverse his condition. Nathan's family decided to withdraw the ventilator. With the support of his physician, the nurse in the intensive care unit, and the chaplain, the family gathered around his bed and the ventilator was turned off. Nathan died peacefully, within minutes.

Do Not Resuscitate (DNR) and Do Not Intubate (DNI)

A "Do Not Resuscitate" (DNR) order is a physician's order stating that a person should not be resuscitated if his or her breathing or heart stops. A "Do Not Intubate" (DNI) order is a physician's order stating that if a person stops breathing, he or she should not have a tube placed down the trachea and should not be connected to a ventilator. DNR and DNI orders are like prescriptions—they require a doctor's signature.

A new term that is gaining popularity is "Allow Natural Death" (AND). Many people prefer this term because it suggests a more peaceful, acceptable image of letting nature run its course.

It is important to remember that DNR and DNI orders are different from advance directives. Even if you state in a healthcare directive that you do not want CPR, most hospitals, nursing facilities, and home care agencies also require a DNR or DNI order.

In the home, DNR and DNI orders should be kept in an obvious location. Many people tape them on the refrigerator or above the bed. In most states, unless a written copy of the order is readily available, medical teams responding to an emergency are required by law to initiate CPR or other life-supporting measures.

Some states will only recognize DNR and DNI orders within a hospital setting (see appendix A). This creates a dilemma if a person is expected to die at home, as is the case with most hospice patients. In this situation, family members often wait several minutes after the death before calling for help. Paramedics are less likely to attempt to revive an obviously dead person.

Comfort Measures

Many people say that it's not illness or dying they fear; it's pain and suffering. Fortunately, incredible advances have been made in treating pain and other symptoms. If your parents would prefer to receive aggressive comfort measures when they are dying, be sure to document these wishes in the healthcare directive. Be as specific as possible.

The following comfort measures neither prolong the dying process nor shorten life:

- medications to manage pain, shortness of breath, anxiety, agitation, insomnia, and other symptoms;
- nonpharmaceutical measures, such as hot or cold packs, acupressure, acupuncture, relaxation exercises and imagery, biofeedback, and Healing Touch;

- oxygen delivered through either a tube that fits under the nostrils or a mask placed over the mouth (oxygen may help with shortness of breath);
- assistance with hygiene, including bathing, oral care, shaving, and clean sheets;
- touch that communicates a caring connection, including light massage, hand holding, foot rubs, and facial massage;
- music to soothe both patient and family (be sure to play music that the patient has always enjoyed);
- prayer; and
- readings from favorite books, poems, and religious writings.

All of these comfort measures may be offered in hospice care, a philosophy of care that focuses on maintaining comfort when a person is dying. Many people specifically request hospice care during the final stages of their lives. See chapter 9 for a complete explanation of hospice.

Although medical technology, with all its wonders, has improved the length and quality of life for millions of people, choosing among various treatments can be confusing and overwhelming. If you and your parents don't understand a particular treatment, ask a doctor or nurse to explain. The more information your parents have, the more likely they are to make informed medical decisions that support their values and goals.

REFERENCES

1. S. J. Diem, J. D. Lantos, and J. A. Tulsky, "Cardiopulmonary Resuscitation on Television: Miracles and Misinformation," *New England Journal of Medicine* 334, no. 24 (1996): 1578–82.

2. R. M. McCann, W. J. Hall, and A. Groth-Juncker, "Comfort Care for Terminally Ill Patients: The Appropriate Use of Nutrition and Hydration," *Journal of the American Medical Association* 272, no. 16 (1994): 1263–66.

3. G. Annas, "How We Lie," *Hasting Center Report* 25, no. 6 (1995): S12–S14.

4

Opening the Discussion

> *First things first, but not necessarily in that order.*
>
> Dr. Who

The coffee is on, the family is gathered, and your anxiety level is soaring. What now? How do you get the conversation going? And how do you get to the issues you really want to discuss?

It may be tempting at this point to pull out the healthcare directive and ask, "So . . . do you want artificial nutrition and hydration?"

Your parents would probably respond, "We'd rather have the cream and sugar first."

In the pages that follow, we offer specific suggestions to help you open a kitchen table discussion. First, however, a few more table manners.

1. Forewarn your parents. Don't just spring the topic on them and expect your parents to be open to an immediate, in-depth discussion about advance care planning. Give them plenty of warning. You might broach the topic through the example of a friend, a relative, or even a stranger you heard about in the news. "Mom, a coworker is going through the hardest time right now. Her father is very ill and she's being asked to make all these really tough decisions because he can't anymore. Her situation makes me think about us, and it occurred to me that I don't really know what you would want. We've never really talked about it before. Do you think we could sit down and do this sometime soon? I would feel so much better knowing that if this ever happens to us, I would be doing what you want me to do."

The death of a public figure can also stimulate conversation. When Hubert Humphrey, former vice president of the United States, died in 1978, it was one of the first well-publicized deaths to occur at home in recent history. The memory is still fresh in the minds of many people. In his stirring eulogy, Walter Mondale said, "He taught us how to live, and in the end, he taught us how to die." Several years ago, Jacqueline Kennedy Onassis also died at home. Simply asking, "Do you remember?" can open up a discussion about what your parents would want at the end of life.

2. Let your parents choose the time and place. The conversation should take place in a setting that is comfortable and familiar to your parents. For many families, the kitchen table is a high comfort zone, or maybe Dad loves his La-z-boy in the living room. Avoid an overly formal setting, which can lead to stiffness and hesitation. Also, the discussion should occur at a time that works best for your parents. If their best time is ten o'clock in the morning, arrange your schedule accordingly.

Sometimes a care planning conversation can happen sponta-
neously. If the topic comes up out of the blue, seize the moment.
For example, Donnie was visiting with her mother, aunt, and
brother, catching up on the family news, when the conversation
turned to Great Aunt Mildred in the nursing home. All of a sudden,
Donnie's mother turned to her and said, "Promise me that you'll
never put me in a nursing home." Soon they were discussing values,
priorities, goals, and fears at the end of life. Donnie said, "I had no
idea that we'd end up talking about all this, but I'd been wanting to
bring it up for months."

If you have the opportunity to seize the moment but do not feel
prepared, it may be best to ask, "Do you have any of this written
down? Can we talk about it more?" and then schedule a time to
talk in the future.

Remember, a kitchen table discussion should be ongoing. You're
unlikely to address all the important issues in just one sitting. And
even if you do, your parents' preferences may change over the
months and years ahead.

3. Come prepared. If you do your homework, the process will
go much more smoothly. First, bring a healthcare directive to the
discussion. Be sure that you are familiar with the format and know
what is needed to make the document legal. Healthcare directives
are usually available at hospitals, home care agencies, nursing
homes, and clinics. They can also be obtained through your state's
Area Agency on Aging. (See chapter 8 and appendix B for more
information about legal documents.)

If you are concerned about some of the changes you are
seeing in your parents' health, make a few phone calls to find out
what kind of support is available. Ask about assistive devices,
community services, or simple home improvements, and bring
this information to your kitchen table discussion. For example, if

you've noticed that Mom is having difficulty preparing meals, you might suggest a Meals-on-Wheels program. If Dad is having a hard time getting up and down the stairs, perhaps a ramp or a chairlift would help. Several national organizations can assist you in locating support. For example, First Call for Help, a service funded by the United Way, operates in many communities across the country. An information clearinghouse, this organization can help you find the resources available in your area. (For more information, see appendix B.)

4. Do not go in with your own agenda. This discussion is about your parents. You may have strong feelings about particular priorities or treatments that you would want for yourself and for those you love, and you may disagree with what your parents believe is right for them. But resist the temptation to argue or debate the merits of any particular thought or opinion. Your first job is to listen and understand. Listen for the needs, wants, and fears your parents are expressing. Try to understand Mom and Dad's history, experience, and perspective.

5. Be a good role model. Advance care planning is not just for those over sixty-five. Stress the importance of this conversation by having your own kitchen table discussion, and consider including your parents. You will find that your credibility is greatly enhanced by your willingness to follow your own advice.

When a colleague in her early thirties was inspired to complete a healthcare directive, she told her parents of the plan. Her parents thought it was a great idea and suggested they have a healthcare directive party. Other family members, including her siblings, aunt, and grandmother, joined in. Not only did they have a valuable discussion, but it turned out to be a great family event.

6. Touch. Families approach the use of touch differently. Touch may be an acceptable way to communicate how you feel about each other, or it may not have played a large role in your family dynamics. An arm around the shoulder, a squeeze of the hand, or a gentle hug can be an effective way of conveying your care and concern. Even if touch is uncomfortable for you or your parents, you may find that a simple gesture such as lightly touching an arm may break down old barriers.

7. Listen. While this is a time to ask questions, it's also a time to listen and learn. As Mark Twain said, "When I was fourteen, my father was so ignorant I could hardly stand to have him around. When I got to be twenty-one, I was astonished at how much he had learned in seven years."

Listening involves more than simply nodding at all the right times. You need to hear what your parents have to say. Simple gestures and phrases can help draw them out. For example:

- Acknowledge what your parents are saying: "It sounds like it was very hard for you when Grandma died."
- Help them clarify their comments: "Are you saying you'd like to go to Disneyland before you have more surgery?"
- Empathize: "I know what you're saying. I felt it too."

How to Break the Ice

Now that we have the rules out of the way, we'll turn our focus to the actual discussion. As we mentioned, anxiety levels will likely be at an all-time high. End-of-life issues can elicit feelings of fear, sadness, even guilt. To break the ice, try asking your parents about their health, their experiences with death, and their fears about healthcare and dying.

Your Parents' Health

Let's say that your once-robust mother no longer insists that you stay for lunch. Or your father has turned over his beloved lawn mower to someone else who can "put it to use." Perhaps your parents are dealing with one or more illnesses. Do you have a good understanding of what is happening? Do they?

The best way to find out is to ask. "Tell me about your health, Dad. What is your understanding of what's going on?" Parents will always be parents, of course, and they may try to protect you from the truth. It's okay to be honest with them. "Dad, I noticed that you have a hard time getting in and out of the car. Are you having problems with your knees?" Or, "Mom, you don't seem to be moving as quickly as you used to. Are you having trouble breathing?" Ask specific questions. This can be uncomfortable, particularly if the news is not good. "What did the doctor tell you about how the treatment is working?"

Children, too, can be guilty of protecting their parents. Louis, a home care social worker tells of the day he helped a patient figure out how to pay for his medications:

When I arrived, the patient's daughter greeted me at the door and said, "He's not doing very well, but please don't talk with him about dying. He might lose hope." I agreed to respect her wishes. When I was taken into the bedroom to see the patient, I saw a very sick man. I asked him, "So, can you tell me what's going on with you?" He looked at me and said, "Isn't it obvious? I'm dying."

Sometimes, what your parents say and what you observe can be entirely different. One hospice social worker remembers being called to the hospital to talk with a man in his early seventies. They sat together as she explained hospice care. He nodded, smiled, and then said, "But I'm not dying. The doctor said he got all the cancer." When she talked with the doctor, he told her, "I explained it all to him. I don't think he wanted to hear it."

If you suspect that your parents are not being realistic, don't hit them over the head with opinions, or even with facts. It's more important to understand how they are feeling. It's also important to be honest with them. "I'm concerned, Mom, because you can't do the things you used to. I want to make sure that I know how you are feeling and what you want."

When straightforward questions don't do the trick, you may want to try a less direct approach. "Tell me what you know about other people who have this condition." It might be easier for Mom to talk about Aunt Myrtle's heart problems than her own.

If you feel that you're not getting clear answers from your parents, offer to accompany them on their next doctor's appointment. If that isn't possible, ask permission to talk with their doctor. This may solidify your understanding of the medical condition. Moreover, you may have information that could be of value to the physician. For example, when John took his mother in for a checkup, he mentioned that she had spent the last year sleeping in a recliner because she had such a hard time breathing. The doctor, who had been completely unaware of this, immediately arranged to have a hospital bed sent to her home.

Remember, physicians and other healthcare professionals are obligated to respect a patient's right to privacy. If you do not have permission from your parents, the doctor should not provide you with medical information. If your parents are comfortable with you hearing their private medical information, ask them to tell their physician.

Your Parents' Experiences with Death

Another great way to begin a kitchen table discussion is to ask your parents about their experiences with death. Even a simple question—for example, "What was it like when Grandma died?"—can get the conversation rolling. Nearly everyone has a story to tell.

Take the example of eighty-eight-year-old Howard. The pain his father experienced in the last days of his life still brings tears to his eyes. "I tried to get Dad to go to the doctor. I remember him doubled over with pain in the living room. I felt so helpless. I don't ever want to be in that kind of pain." From that brief reminiscence, it is clear that pain control is one of Howard's priorities.

Jeanie tells another kind of story. "It isn't always about not doing treatments. When my grandma was dying, I felt like the hospital gave up on her. We had to fight to get the tests and treatments we thought she should have." For Jeanie, it is important to know that someone will serve as an advocate for her.

Art talks about his cousin. "He lay there for years in a nursing home being fed through a tube and not knowing anybody. I wouldn't want to spend the rest of my life as a vegetable." It's clear that Art does not want extraordinary measures taken to keep him alive.

When Alberta was diagnosed with lung cancer, she opted for no treatment. She told her children, "Remember all the years that Dad was sick? I don't want to put you through that. I'm eighty-four years old, and when it's my time, it's my time."

Your Parents' Fears about Healthcare and Dying

Alberta's husband had died in a nursing home after many years of declining health from Parkinson's disease. "I was there every day for him, but I don't want my family to go through that." It is clear that one of Alberta's greatest fears is dying in a nursing home.

We all have fears, some rational and some not. Your parents may be at a stage in their lives where most of their fears revolve around health, death, and end-of-life care. A 1997 Gallup poll asked, "What worries you when you think about your own death?" The responses:[1]

- The possibility of being a vegetable for some period of time (73 percent);
- Not having a chance to say goodbye to someone (73 percent);
- The possibility of great physical pain (67 percent);
- How my loved ones will be cared for (65 percent);
- That my death will cause inconvenience and stress for those who love me (64 percent).

When starting a kitchen table discussion, an important question to ask is, "What do you fear?" This can open the door to a conversation about care preferences. In Alberta's case, it was the start of a discussion about hospice care.

Jody learned about her father's fears when she talked to him about his older brother, Kent. For years, Kent had received kidney dialysis due to advanced diabetes. Jody's dad also had diabetes, and he, too, faced the possibility of dialysis. She was quite surprised, and somewhat distressed, to learn that her father was adamantly opposed to beginning dialysis:

I had to bite my tongue and fight the urge to demand that he go on dialysis if and when the time came. He's got four grandkids I want him to be there for, and I'm not ready to be without a dad. But then he started talking about Uncle Kent and the fear he had been holding onto for years: that he, too, would have to go through the same thing. Dad told me that

*Uncle Kent was miserable and often said that if he had it to do over
again, he would never choose the dialysis. Dad was afraid of having the
same thing happen to him. I'm so glad I let him talk.*

Sometimes parents reveal their fears indirectly. Rachel, a nurse,
talks about a comment her father-in-law made when he was in
failing health:

*One day he said to me, "Do you know how to get ahold of this Dr.
Kervorkian?" My first thought was, "Don't be silly." Instead, I asked him
what he wanted with Dr. Kervorkian. It turned out that he was worried
about a multitude of things, including becoming a burden to his family,
being in severe pain, and possibly having to move to a nursing home. It
gave me a deeper understanding of the distress he was experiencing, and
it was the beginning of a really helpful conversation between him and the
rest of the family.*

Whether we agree with his approach or not, Dr. Jack Kervorkian
has stimulated conversations around the country about end-of-life
issues. He is well known for his work in assisting patients in their
suicides. Many chronically or terminally ill people are attracted to
the promise of an end to their suffering. If your parents begin to
talk about assisted suicide, it's extremely important to listen to
what they have to say. They might reveal their fears and worries
about the future.

What If My Parents Resist?

If you sense hesitation or outright resistance when you first bring
up the topic of advance care planning, you may feel inclined to drop
the subject. Again, saying things out loud can make them less scary:
"I sense that this is making you uncomfortable. I have to admit,
I was nervous about bringing it up. But I believe strongly that this is
important for us to do. Please think about it and let's talk about it

later." Reassure your parents that you want to talk about these things because you love them and want the best for them.

Recognize that this is a difficult topic. Ask your parents if they are afraid of anything in particular, or whether something is keeping them from being able to discuss it.

Martin, an elderly gentleman with severe lung disease, had been placed on a ventilator twice for breathing problems. Given his fragile state of health, his family wanted to talk about care planning and complete a healthcare directive, but he staunchly refused. Martin worried that an advance directive meant nothing would be done for him in a medical crisis. He said, "I've been at death's door twice and I'm still here. I want them to do whatever they can to keep me going." When the social worker explained that an advance directive is used to communicate one's wishes regarding medical treatments, both in applying them and withholding them, Martin was eager to discuss his wishes and complete the directive.

The following phrases might decrease your parents' resistance to a kitchen table discussion:

- Have you thought about writing down the kind of care you would want if you were terminally ill?
- Have you thought about the care you would want if you couldn't speak for yourself?
- Making decisions before a crisis is a gift you can give to us.
- We need to know what to say to the doctors if you can't say it yourself.
- I've had this talk with my own family.
- This is like buying life insurance; it's a way of planning for the future.

Funeral Planning

If you are trying to have a kitchen table discussion, and all Mom wants to talk about is her funeral, don't stop the conversation with: "Sorry, Mom, I'm only interested in whether you want CPR. The funeral will have to wait."

Many people who are reluctant to talk about end-of-life care are perfectly comfortable planning their funeral. This can be a backdoor to a conversation about care wishes and goals, as well as an excellent opportunity to find out what kind of planning has been done.

A friend who recently lost her mother-in-law said, "I was amazed to find out that both my mother-in-law and father-in-law had sat down with a funeral director over five years ago to prepay and pre-plan their funerals. I was particularly surprised to discover that this was my mother-in-law's idea. She never wanted to talk about death."

Your parents may see funeral planning as a gift they can give to you. As one elderly man put it, "I don't want my children to have to fuss over that." This is your opportunity to say, "Thanks for seeing to this. Now you can help us out again by talking about your care preferences in case the time comes when you can't speak for yourself."

If your parents would like to document their funeral wishes, some healthcare directives include a section on funeral planning. This is a great opportunity to talk about the type of service Mom or Dad would want and to put their wishes in writing, including:

- place of service;
- specific requests, such as music or readings;
- preference for cremation or burial;
- preference for final resting place;
- information to include in the obituary; and
- information for the death certificate, such as birth date and birthplace.

If you are looking for more information on funeral planning, the Funeral Service Educational Foundation provides a pamphlet entitled "Making Funeral Arrangements." (For order information, see appendix B.) You can also contact your local funeral director.

REFERENCES

1. Survey, October 1997 (George H. Gallup Institute for the Nathan Cummings Foundation and Fetzer Institute).

5

Understanding Values and Goals

If I'd known I was going to live this long,
I'd have taken better care of myself.

Eubie Blake

Once you have opened the conversation, the next step is to understand what is truly important to your parents. What do they value? What are they looking forward to? What are their important relationships? This information will give you a deeper understanding of the reasons behind their healthcare goals.

Seventy-four-year-old Bernie had been an Olympic athlete in his youth. He was very proud of his body. When his health failed and he lost circulation in one of his legs, his doctor said, "We will have to amputate, or you will die." Bernie knew that the amputation would only buy him a little more time. He said, "I want to leave this life with my body whole." Because his family knew how important this was to him, they supported his decision to not have the amputation. Bernie died at home under hospice care. His son later said, "This was hard. I wanted to keep him with us as long as possible, but Dad wouldn't have wanted to be mutilated like that. I'm glad we knew what was important to him."

When talking about values and goals, remember your table manners. This is not meant to be a family therapy session. It is not the time to confront Mom on why it was so important to her that you take piano lessons, or find out why Dad always made you stand in the corner when it was sister Suzie's fault. The conversation needs to stay focused on how you can honor and respect your parents' healthcare decisions.

Values

The American Heritage Dictionary defines a value as "a principle, standard, or quality considered worthwhile or desirable." Values influence the choices we make. Questions about values can be as straightforward as:

- What do you value most in life?
- What makes life worth living?
- What will be most important to you when you are dying?
- If you were to die soon, what would be left undone in your life?

The values most likely to influence your parents' healthcare decisions include family, money, independence, and spirituality.

Family

Many people view family as the most important factor in their lives. For this reason, family matters often have a powerful influence on healthcare decisions. Wally, for example, felt a sense of completion when he talked about his family. "I've lived a good life. I have a wonderful family. I'm very fortunate that I never had to bury a child or a grandchild. When it's my time to go, I'm ready."

When family business goes unresolved, however, people are more likely to pursue aggressive, life-prolonging treatment. A home care social worker relates an encounter she had with a man in his seventies:

Simon knew his time was short, but he still wanted to try more treatments. When I asked him if he had any uncompleted business, he explained that he wanted to be reunited with a foster son he hadn't seen in many years. "I just need to know he's okay," he said.

Family relationships can determine where a person would want to be cared for if he or she were dying. Wally was very clear about this: "At home, if at all possible." He wanted to be somewhere that was comfortable for him and for his loved ones. Another person might feel differently: "In a nursing home, so I won't be a burden to my family."

Don't forget other relationships that might influence healthcare decisions. For example, you may not think of Dad's poodle as family, but Dad might make some decisions based on his worries about little Bowser. "I can't possibly have that surgery. Who would take care of Bowser?" This is the time to work out some of the "what ifs" and reassure Dad that Bowser would be well cared for.

Money

The value your parents place on money and finances can also have a tremendous affect on their healthcare decisions. National surveys have shown that one of the greatest fears people have at the end of life is becoming a financial burden to their loved ones. A person's healthcare decisions can be greatly affected by the fear of losing a "nest egg" or becoming financially dependent.

For those who grew up during the Depression, frugality may be a way of life. As one exasperated son said, "The doctor ordered hospice care for Mom, but she wouldn't let them in the door. She was afraid that it would cost too much. Even when I told her it was covered under Medicare, she said, 'I don't want any charity from the county.' I couldn't convince her otherwise."

Independence

Independence, too, can be a strong personal value. A ninety-two-year-old widower said he would rather die than lose his independence. "I've always taken care of myself. I don't want to be helpless and in a nursing home like my wife was."

To some people, independence means physical autonomy; for others, it is mental clarity. Donna tells the story of her father and his decision about resuscitation prior to a risky surgery:

Dad's health was terrible. He had multiple problems and he'd been going downhill for quite some time. The doctors said he needed abdominal surgery. To my amazement, when they asked him about resuscitation, he said, "Absolutely. If my heart stops, I want CPR. As long as I've still got my brain, I want to keep going."

Spirituality

Spiritual or faith-based values can be a crucial factor in healthcare decisions. For some people, decisions about medical treatment carry deep religious implications. A hospital chaplain recounts a dying woman's decision about life support:

She had a widespread cancer that was affecting her ability to breathe. The doctors offered to put her on a ventilator, but they strongly discouraged it. The patient chose the ventilator, saying, "If it's there for me, then it's God's will that I use it." She died several days later in the intensive care unit, on the ventilator.

For some people, when it comes down to specific treatment choices, such as foregoing life support, it's important to have input from trusted clergy. Bill talks about his mother, who was raised in a traditional Catholic family:

She was afraid that if she didn't choose to have all the possible treatments, she would be breaking the laws of the church. It was very helpful to have her priest talk with her and assure her that the church did not view it that way.

Goals

Healthcare goals are influenced as much by personal goals as they are by personal values. If Dad has always wanted to see the Grand Canyon, he'll probably want every possible treatment in the event of a heart attack. But if Dad is experiencing heart failure and the Grand Canyon is no longer doable, his main goal might be to stay out of the coronary care unit.

Healthcare goals can range from "I want to live as long as I can" to "I don't want to ever be in the hospital again." At the end of life, however, individuals may have very different goals. According to a new study, dying people want:[1]

- comfort and pain relief;
- preparation for death (knowing what to expect);
- a sense of completion in their lives (through resolving conflicts, spending time with friends and family, and saying goodbye); and
- acknowledgment that even though they are dying, they still have a lot to contribute to others.

Discussing end-of-life goals with your parents can be difficult. Whether or not your parents are in ill health, try to get a handle on their hopes for the future. Ask, "Where would you like to see yourself in the next week, next month, next year? What are your goals for the future?" If the word "goal" doesn't work, simply ask, "What do you hope for?"

Keep in mind that goals change over time. At one point, your terminally ill father might say, "I'm going to take every treatment offered if it will ensure that I can stand up at my granddaughter's wedding." After the wedding, avoiding pain may be his number one goal. Mom might want to live long enough to see her grandson graduate from college, but after that, she may want to live to see her first great-grandchild. Remember your table manners: This is an ongoing discussion.

Imposing Your Values

Even if you disagree with your parents' choices, beliefs, and goals, it's important to talk about their values—and yours. Only after reaching a mutual understanding will you be able to respect and honor your parents' wishes. Never impose your values on your parents.

Consider Shelly, a thirty-year-old woman wrestling with her grandmother's decision to quit taking nourishment:

Grandma seemed very comfortable with the decision. She was relieved that she would no longer struggle with choking whenever she tried to swallow. I kept offering food and pleading, "But we can't just starve you, Grandma." Finally, after watching her choke on a sip of coffee, I came to terms with her decision.

In another scenario, thirty-seven-year-old Leslie had taken care of her bedridden grandmother for several years without ever knowing what made her grandmother's life important:

One day, Grandmother said to a visiting nurse, "I just love my life here. Look, I have my bed by the window so I can see out. I have my cat. And I have my family around me. I'm certainly not ready to die!" I was really surprised to hear that, and I'll remember those words the next time she gets sick. As long as she sees her life as good, I want to keep it that way.

Resources to Help You Understand Your Parents' Values

A Family Caregiver's Guide to Planning and Decision Making for the Elderly, by James A. Wilkinson, contains an excellent worksheet called a "Values History Form." The questions on this form relate to overall attitudes toward life, health, and personal relationships; thoughts about independence and self-sufficiency; and feelings about illness, dying, finances, and funeral plans. You might consider using this form as a springboard for an in-depth discussion.

The Ethical Will Resource Kit, by Barry Baines, MD, offers a different perspective on values and relationships. Ethical wills come from an old Jewish tradition of leaving a legacy of values to the next generation. In modern form, it is an opportunity for your parents to write down the experiences, ideas, and thoughts that they feel are important to pass on. This resource offers examples and exercises to help your parents begin the writing process. Below is an ethical will written by a seventy-year-old man to his son and daughter-in-law. He died a month after he wrote it:[2]

Dear Keith and Leigh,

A few words to express my feelings and thoughts while time is running out on me.

Some standard values that I have basically lived by throughout my life, are that I have always believed in honesty and advocated truthfulness. I cherish the family with all my heart. I always felt that I gave of myself to everyone in the family. The satisfaction and gratification that I received in return is in the accomplishments of my children. No father could be as proud as your father is of you. Throughout your lifetime so far, you have more than exceeded my greatest expectations. You continue to move forward in a manner that makes me love you more and more. I'm proud to say "that's my son!"

Through the years, I've tried to take care of my family and give them some of the better things in life. I tried and succeeded in being able to give my children a good education. Although I was only a working man, many was the time I worked two jobs for the extra money so that the family could have a little bit more. I had often thought of going into some kind of business, but I didn't have the expertise in any particular field, or the finances to afford the luxury of risk. However, I'm proud to say that you have shown me through the years, the aggressiveness that I lacked emerged in you.

I have tried to be financially sound and leave behind an adequate amount of finances to carry your mother through the rest of her days. Being no one can predict the future, I ask that should it ever be necessary, see that your mother remains comfortable financially and otherwise.

Leigh, you have always made me proud with your accomplish-ments and different endeavors. You have never undertaken a task that was under-achieved. Through the years you have been in my confidence and as close as a daughter. I love you and the girls deeply.

My concentration is not too great at this point as I'm sure I can say much more. Keith could not have picked a finer mate. You are a good wife and excellent mother. I feel a father and daughter relation to you. I hope Danielle and Michelle follow in the footsteps of the family and their traditions. I love you all.

Dad

REFERENCES

1. K. E. Steinhauser, et al., "In Search of a Good Death: Observations of Patients, Families and Providers," *Annals of Internal Medicine* 132, no. 10 (May 2000): 825–31.

2. From http://www.ethicalwill.com. Accessed August 2000. Used with permission.

6

Assessing Decision-Making Ability

My life has a superb cast, but I can't figure out the plot.
Ashleigh Brilliant

Suppose the family is gathered expectantly around Mom's kitchen table. You're using all the tricks to start the conversation, but Mom just looks at you with a blank smile. When you ask her what's wrong, she says, "I wonder what happened to the coffeepot. I think someone must have stolen it."

In a moment of panic, you think, "If Mom can't remember where she put the coffeepot, is she capable of talking about health-care options and goals?" The answer is in the gray zone—usually yes, but sometimes no.

Consider these very common scenarios:

- Mom's gotten so forgetful lately. I was visiting last week and she forgot to turn the oven off after dinner. We didn't discover it until the next morning.
- Dad's had so many health problems in the last few years. He's lost so much of his independence, and he's gotten really depressed. He talks about how he doesn't want to be kept alive and that he's done with life. But is that what he really wants?
- Lately when I see Dad at the nursing home, he doesn't always recognize me right away. Once he does, it's like his memory kicks back in and he's fine. He'll even ask about things, like my daughter's basketball game or my son's job. I'd like to talk about advance care planning, but there's no telling how "with it" he might be.

Are Your Parents Competent?

One of the assumptions in a healthcare directive is that the person completing the directive is in his or her "right mind." When your parents display behaviors that make you question their competence, how should you proceed?

"Decision-making capacity" is a common phrase used in the legal and medical community. With regard to medical care, it means the ability to understand the significant benefits, risks, and alternatives to proposed healthcare, and to make and communicate a healthcare decision.

The process of determining decision-making capacity is not black and white. If you notice a change in behavior or if your parents seem confused, get them to the doctor for a thorough examination.

Some changes are treatable. For example, Gwen noticed that her father was getting more forgetful. When she looked in the medicine cabinet, she discovered that he was on eleven different medications. She brought him to the doctor, who sorted through all his pills and whittled them down to three "essentials." Within two weeks, the confusion had cleared up.

Mental impairment can be permanent or temporary. Causes of impairment include:

- physical trauma (accident, stroke, surgery);
- blood loss;
- depression;
- mental illness;
- infection;
- interaction of medications; and
- metabolic disorder.

Healthcare professionals have a few tools that they use to assess the mental status of patients. The Mini-Mental Status exam is used to determine the extent of cognitive (thinking) impairment. The Functional Assessment Staging Test (FAST) assesses behavioral impairment, which might range from minor forgetfulness to more serious complaints, such as difficulty performing complex tasks or making simple choices.

Of course, the inability to count backward by threes, balance one's checkbook, or remember today's date does not mean that a person is incapable of having a meaningful conversation about advance care planning. While tests can be helpful, they cannot determine if a person is capable of understanding potential health scenarios and options for life-support treatment. In a study of nursing home residents with progressive physical and cognitive disabilities, 90 percent of residents with severe cognitive impairment were able to answer "yes" or "no" to questions regarding a health-care agent. In fact, half of these residents were able to specifically name an agent.[1]

If your parents are mentally impaired, healthcare discussions must be specific rather than broad, and presented at a level that your parents will understand. Talk about treatment alternatives, such as tube feedings or a breathing machine, rather than the broader concept of life support. Also, expect variation in your parents' ability to comprehend particular treatments. Dad might easily understand the idea of having a feeding tube put down his nose, but he may be unable to grasp the concept of dialysis (being hooked up to a blood-cleaning machine). To ensure that your parents have understood the information, ask them to describe what the specific treatment involves and what would happen if the treatment were not given: "Tell me what you understand about feeding tubes and what would happen if you did not have one."

A doctor relates this story about one of her nursing home patients:

Clara, an elderly woman with dementia and advanced lung disease, had completed a healthcare directive a couple years ago when she was thinking clearly. It stated that she did not want to be resuscitated or placed on a breathing machine. Clara frequently told her family, the nursing home staff, and me that she wanted to die. But when she became short of breath, she begged the nurses at the nursing home to "do something." They sent her to the hospital. Clara continued to voice these seemingly opposing pleas: "Let me die" and "Do something." Once I explained the alternatives in simple, straightforward language, Clara was able to clearly—and adamantly—communicate what she wanted. She did not want to be placed on a machine to breathe, but she did want to be given medication and oxygen so that she would not feel short of breath. I was able to accommodate both of her requests without conflict.

Depression

It is not uncommon for people to become depressed during the course of an illness. Depression does not necessarily impair decision-making capacity, but it can cloud a person's ability to understand information and communicate preferences. If you or the doctor suspect that depression is affecting Mom or Dad's ability to make healthcare decisions, a psychiatrist should be called in for a consultation. It is important to determine if your parent can comprehend the pros and cons of treatment and communicate a decision. This applies to people with other mental illnesses as well, such as schizophrenia or bipolar disease.

Be Patient with Your Parents

Obviously, if Mom or Dad's mental status is somewhat impaired, a meaningful kitchen table discussion will probably take more time and energy on everyone's part. Don't expect to complete the discussion in one sitting. Stop if you see signs of fatigue or agitation.

Jim, a home care social worker, talks of advance care planning with an elderly woman who has dementia:

Suddenly she started shaking her head and hands and said, "I can't sit here. I need to move around." She stood up quickly, grabbed her walker, and began to shuffle around in circles. Even though she could not verbalize it, our discussion was beginning to upset her. I allowed her to expend some nervous energy and then drew her attention to the intricate, framed needle-point pictures on the wall, knowing that this hobby was her pride and joy. Her energies diverted to a more comfortable topic, she calmed down immediately. I did not resume the discussion during this visit, other than to set up another time to continue the conversation. At future appointments, I lowered my expectations regarding how much we would be able to discuss.

While you don't want to rush your parents through a kitchen table discussion, you need to begin advance care planning before it's too late to have a meaningful conversation. Remember the elephant in the living room. When you begin to see signs of mental decline, act as quickly as you can to discuss healthcare wishes, fill out a healthcare directive, and appoint the healthcare agent.

REFERENCES

1. P. A. Singer, et al, "Reconceptualizing Advance Care Planning from the Patient's Perspective," *Archives of Internal Medicine* 158 (1998): 879–84.

7

How to Talk with the Doctor

*It should be the function of medicine to help
people die young as late in life as possible.*

Dr. Ernst Wunder

Suppose you have lots of questions, and you want to include Dr. Smith in your kitchen table discussion. You jump up from the table, go to the phone, and call.

"Say, Dr. Smith, we're having a conversation about advance care planning. Do you think you could stop by for a little pie and coffee? We have some questions."

The most likely response you'll get from Dr. Smith's answering service is, "Huh?"

If Dr. Smith can't come to your kitchen table discussion, consider bringing the discussion to Dr. Smith. (The pie is optional.) This is a good opportunity to talk about the care preferences you've been discussing, and the doctor can offer advice and wisdom on what's happening with Mom or Dad.

Which Doctor?

First, of course, you need to figure out which doctor to include in your discussion.

Ask your parents if they have a doctor you can talk to. If the answer is yes, skip ahead to the next section, "How to Prepare for the Visit," on page 83. If the answer is no, it's time to find a doctor.

The following questions are helpful when choosing a physician:[1]

- Is the doctor accepting new patients?
- How far in advance are appointments made?
- How quickly are emergency visits handled, and who sees emergency patients?
- Who takes care of patients after-hours?
- To what hospital does the doctor admit patients?
- Does the doctor see patients at home? At a nursing home?
- Which insurance or health plans does the doctor accept?
- Where is the office located? Is it close enough to home?

Also, is the doctor a generalist or a specialist? Generalists, such as internists, family practitioners, or geriatricians, are trained to handle a wide variety of symptoms and conditions. Specialists, such as cardiologists and oncologists, work with a particular disease or condition. Many people see several specialists but do not see a generalist on a regular basis. In this case, a specialist who has a long-standing relationship with your parents may agree to be considered their primary care physician.

Try to avoid a situation where no one is in charge of your parents' care. If several doctors are involved, it's possible to have conflicting opinions and treatments. A "primary" doctor can help you sort through the recommendations to determine what's best for Mom or Dad.

Raymond, a healthcare professional, explains how care can become confusing when several doctors are involved:

I was at a family gathering when I met my brother's friend Melanie. She was thin and frail and walked as if she were in a lot of pain. My brother mentioned that she was being treated for ovarian cancer. When I told her I was a nurse, she told me about her pain. "My oncologist gave me morphine, but my internist said I shouldn't have it." She added, "I'm also having these shooting pains down my back. The neurologist gave me some pills for it, but the nephrologist said they might damage my kidneys."

I was so overwhelmed by how complicated her medical care had become that I finally asked her, "But who would you call if you woke up in the middle of the night with terrible pain?" She looked at me and said, "Why, that would depend on where the pain was. If it was here," she said, pointing to her abdomen, "I'd call my internist. If it was here," she said, pointing to her back, "I'd call my neurologist."

How to Prepare for the Visit

Doctors are busier than ever these days, so once you've scheduled an appointment with a physician, you'll want to use his or her time wisely. A few pointers:

- **Schedule a long appointment.** Explain to the scheduler that you want to talk about your parents' healthcare directive and will need a little more time than usual.

- **Let your parents do the talking.** Unless they defer to you, your job will be to clarify information and keep the discussion on track.

- **Consider bringing a tape recorder.** With a conversation as important as this, it is crucial to remember everything that is said. If you record the discussion, you'll be able to clarify or confirm specific information, and family members will have a chance to hear the conversation for themselves. Of course, it's a good idea to explain to the doctor why you are doing this and to obtain his or her consent before recording the conversation.

- **Come with an agenda.** Discuss with your parents the topics you would like to cover, and make sure they are comfortable with the agenda: "Dad, can we talk about your heart condition and what we might expect in the coming months?" or "Mom, I know it's important that your pain be controlled. Can we discuss this with the doctor and make sure she knows what you want?"

- **Organize your questions and concerns into categories:** what you need to know, what the doctor needs to know, what your options are, and what the doctor recommends.

During the Visit

Your parents should have a frank and open discussion with the doctor about their current health, treatment options, advance care wishes, and healthcare directives. Ideally, the doctor will be honest, give clear answers, and prepare your parents for what is to come. You can encourage this conversation by clarifying key points:

- Dr. Smith, can you tell us what will happen after surgery?"
- Dad, did you understand what Dr. Smith just said?
- Mom, Dr. Smith recommends you stop the treatment. Is that what you want?

When the time is right, bring out your notes. Ask your questions and share as much information as you can.

What Do We Need to Know?

Questions like this encompass a multitude of issues ranging from "How long have I got?" to "Will I lose my independence?" and "Can I expect a lot of pain?" Most people want at least a general picture of what to expect in the coming weeks, months, and years.

Keep in mind, prognostication is a tricky issue for physicians. Although it is reasonable to ask, "Doc, how long have I got?" there isn't always an easy answer. Even hospice professionals who work with dying patients on a daily basis can't always make accurate predictions. Loren talks about his Aunt Betty:

Aunt Betty was living with us and receiving hospice care because of her bad heart. When she caught a cold that turned into pneumonia, she was confined to bed. She struggled to breathe. The hospice nurses told us it wouldn't be long, maybe another week. The whole family was prepared, ready to gather around the deathbed. One morning, Aunt Betty woke up and said, "I think I'm feeling better." A week later, she was out of bed. A month later, she was doing so well that she was discharged from the hospice program. That was two years ago. Aunt Betty is still with us.

Although the doctor may not be able to give you the exact date and time, he or she should be able to offer more than "God only knows." Regardless of the doctor's uncertainty, it's always reasonable to ask.

What Does the Doctor Need to Know?

The doctor should be told about the values, wishes, and goals that your parents expressed during the kitchen table discussion. Perhaps Dad's priorities are to avoid pain, die at home, and do nothing to prolong his life. Or he might have stated a very different set of goals: "I want to beat this disease so I can travel like I've always planned. I'm willing to try any kind of new treatment you can find." This information will help the doctor make informed recommendations for the healthcare directive. It can also help determine Dad's future course of treatment.

What Are Our Options?

Most of our parents grew up in an era when doctors were not questioned. Patients did what they were told. Over the last twenty years, however, patients' rights and individual responsibility have become important factors in the doctor-patient relationship.

When an obvious treatment will cure a disease, a doctor is unlikely to say, "Here, you decide: You can have your appendix removed and live, or you can skip it and die a horrible death from peritonitis." Instead, the doctor will explain: "The next step will be to take out your appendix."

When treatment is not so clear-cut, however, a doctor may offer a menu of choices. Of course, getting the best healthcare is not the same as walking into a restaurant and choosing between a cheeseburger and a chef's salad. When considering medical treatment options, remember that the doctor is the expert in disease and pathology. You are meeting with him or her for that expertise. If your doctor offers a list of options, the following questions will help you and your parents make an informed choice:

- Why would we want treatment A over treatment B?
- Given Dad's priorities and wishes, what do you recommend?
- Does this treatment make sense considering Mom's overall condition?
- What would you choose under the circumstances?

This is also the time to discuss particular treatment choices and other issues. "What does resuscitation mean? Would it make sense for Mom?" or "If Dad decides to go on dialysis, what will his life look like?" or "Sometimes Mom and Dad talk about stopping their pills. If they did, what would happen?"

What Are the Doctor's Recommendations?

The doctor-patient relationship should be one of mutual respect. If your parents are struggling with a choice between various treatment options, it's reasonable to ask the doctor for help in making the best decision. Good, two-way communication is key to the doctor-patient relationship.

Keep the following points in mind when asking the doctor for recommendations:

- **Doctors often speak in highly technical language.** It's appropriate to ask, "Can you explain this in a way that we will understand?"
- **Doctors are human.** For some physicians, talking about end-of-life issues can be uncomfortable. It's okay to say, "We need you to be honest about this," or to ask, "What does a 10 percent chance really mean?"
- **Although medical treatments can have great benefits, they can pose certain risks and burdens.** In addition to offering diagnoses and treatments, a physician can help

you weigh the risks, benefits, and other consequences. For example, if the doctor suggests a test that involves hospitalization or some amount of discomfort, it's okay to ask, "What will you do with the test results? Will they make a difference in the treatment or prognosis? Will they help us to better understand the course of this illness?"

The Follow-Up

Like a kitchen table discussion, consulting with a doctor can be an ongoing process. Perhaps you need time to absorb the information. Perhaps you want to wait awhile to see how the situation plays out. Or perhaps the doctor was not able to answer all of your questions during your appointment.

Chances are you'll need to make a follow-up appointment. Start with a phone call: "We've thought it over, and we want to start treatment as soon as possible" or "We appreciate your time in meeting with us last week. After going over our options, we have a few more questions."

During your follow-up, give the doctor a copy of your parents' healthcare directive, if you haven't already. Review the directive together, then ask the doctor to keep it on file at the medical facility. It's very important that the doctor knows and understands your parents' choices. If your parents have several doctors who are frequently involved in their care, make sure all of them have a copy of the healthcare directive.

REFERENCES

1. *Talking with Your Doctor: A Guide for Older People* (Gaithersburg, Md.: National Institute on Aging, 1998).

8

Completing a Healthcare Directive

> *The job's not finished until the paperwork is done.*
>
> Anonymous

Goals and preferences have been discussed, the doctor consulted, the options explained. It is now time for the healthcare directive. At this point, your kitchen table discussion will likely focus on "what ifs."

What kind of care would your parents want if they were at the end stages of a terminal illness? What if they were in a serious accident, where recovery was possible but unlikely? What if they went into the hospital for minor surgery, but serious complications developed? Any healthcare professional who has worked in a hospital, especially in the intensive care unit, can attest to the unforeseen complications that regularly present themselves. Infections develop, organs fail, drug reactions occur. Every person is unique, every body is different, and people with the same condition may respond differently to the same treatment.

When writing their healthcare directives, your parents will want to consider the most common scenarios that people encounter at the end of life.

Scenario 1: They have a terminal illness with no reasonable expectation of recovery. Death is imminent. (Think in terms of incurable cancer in the final stages.) No further treatment would arrest, reverse, or cure the illness.

Scenario 2: They are suffering from a chronic, progressive illness that will eventually lead to death. This would include congestive heart failure, chronic obstructive pulmonary disease, chronic kidney failure, and cirrhosis of the liver. It would also include progressive neuromuscular conditions such as ALS, Parkinson's disease, and multiple sclerosis. When writing a healthcare directive, remember that many people who live with these conditions can think of "states worse than death" that they would prefer not to endure.

Scenario 3: They are permanently unconscious or in a persistent vegetative state (the irreversible loss of bodily function, which requires artificial life support). Death may or may not be imminent. Because they are immobile, people in this state are at high risk for bedsores and infections such as pneumonia. You may remember the highly publicized cases of Karen Ann Quinlan in the 1970s and Nancy Cruzan in the early 1990s; both individuals were in a permanent vegetative state.

Scenario 4: They have a serious, acute, or devastating illness or injury for which there is no reasonable expectation of recovery. This scenario refers to unpredictable, nonchronic conditions such as infectious disease or multiple injuries resulting from an accident.

What differs in this scenario is the "ray of hope," the possibility that some type of therapy may be effective. Treatment may indeed save the person's life, but it may come at a cost to long-term quality of life.

How to Fill Out the Directive

All fifty states, as well as the District of Columbia, will recognize healthcare directives, healthcare agents, or both (see appendix A). There are many kinds of healthcare directives, and each state has its own requirements. The laws are constantly changing, so check with your local Area Agency on Aging for the current laws in your state. Partnership for Caring, another organization that can tell you about your state laws, offers state-specific healthcare directive forms (see the resources section at the end of this book).

Before putting pen to paper, consider the following tips:

- **A healthcare directive should never be filled out alone.** As we have emphasized, the value of a kitchen table discussion is in sharing and clarifying preferences. A written directive, no matter how well written, is of no use if no one knows about it.
- **Be flexible.** Whatever is written can be changed as goals and preferences change.
- **Healthcare directives vary from state to state.** See appendix A for information about your state's laws.
- **Do not write instructions asking for treatments that are illegal in your state.** This includes assisted suicide, mercy killing, or euthanasia. Such instructions could jeopardize the legality of the document, and in some cases render it useless.

Most healthcare directives have three parts:

- instructions for healthcare goals and treatment preferences;
- the designation of a healthcare agent; and
- signatures to make it legal.

Instructions for Healthcare Goals and Treatment Preferences

In this section of the healthcare directive, your parents can make statements about their personal values and goals (as discussed in chapter 5). For example, from a seventy-seven-year-old man with multiple health problems:

I've lived a long and good life. I have a wonderful, loving family. I value them above all else. When my time comes, I am ready to die. I do not want any treatments that would prolong my life. I do want to be kept comfortable and as pain-free as possible. I would like to have my care in my own home, if possible. If not, I want to be in a place where my family can be at my side.

From a forty-five-year-old woman undergoing treatment for breast cancer:

I believe that I still have some important things to accomplish in my life. I want to live as long as I can in order to finish my business here on earth. I would like treatments that would prolong my life and assure me as much time as possible with my family. If, however, I reach a point where treatment is no longer effective and would interfere with the time I have with my family, I want it to be discontinued.

From an eighty-two-year-old widow with lung disease:

I have strong faith in God. I believe that if I am in a condition where I can no longer tell people my wishes, He will be my comfort. Therefore, I do not want life-supporting measures. I want to die naturally, in God's time.

In addition to a statement about values and goals, your parents can specify which treatments they want and which they don't want. If Mom is clear that she doesn't want to be resuscitated under any circumstances, then make sure her directive says "DNR" or "no resuscitation." If Dad does not want a tube down his throat or to be placed on a ventilator, make sure his directive says "DNI" or "no intubation or mechanical ventilation." (In the case of DNR and DNI, a healthcare directive may not be sufficient. Again, most healthcare facilities have policies that require CPR when a patient's heart or breathing stops. If your parents do not want this treatment, a doctor's order is required. Do not assume that a DNR or DNI preference will be honored just because it is written in the healthcare directive and the directive is in the patient's chart. Ask for a specific doctor's order.)

The most common treatment preferences addressed in a healthcare directive are the following:

- CPR (cardiopulmonary resuscitation);
- DNR and DNI (Do Not Resuscitate and Do Not Intubate) orders;
- mechanical ventilation;
- artificial nutrition and hydration;
- dialysis;
- blood transfusions;
- antibiotics; and
- surgery.

An organization called Aging with Dignity provides an on-line healthcare directive titled "Five Wishes" (www.agingwithdignity.org). Valid in thirty-six states, Five Wishes lists all of these life-supporting treatments and allows individuals to pick and choose the treatments they would want to have at the end of life. If you do not use the Five

Wishes form, the following statements may help your parents specify treatment preferences:

- I do not want artificial life support to be initiated, and if it is, I want it to be discontinued.
- I want all appropriate and medically indicated life-support treatment.
- I want the following life-support treatments, if medically appropriate and feasible. . . .
- I [do not] want resuscitation or CPR.
- I [do not] want to be placed on a ventilator.
- I [do not] want to be fed by a tube placed either through my nose or directly into my stomach.
- I [do not] want to be placed on dialysis.
- In case of infection, I [do not] want to be treated with antibiotics.
- I [do not] want blood transfusions.
- I want my pain and suffering to be treated aggressively to bring me comfort and relief from my symptoms.
- I want a trial of therapy for a reasonable time, to be determined by my healthcare agent and physician. If it should be determined that such treatment is ineffective or excessively burdensome, then I want all artificial life support to be discontinued.

In order to be effective, treatment preferences need to be clear to anyone who reads them. For example, the phrase "no heroic measures" might look good on paper, but what does it mean? One doctor might interpret "heroic measures" to mean CPR; another might think it means surgery or the use of antibiotics.

Brian, a hospice coordinator, relates his confusion over a vague healthcare directive:

The directive said, "I want short-term resuscitation." But CPR is an all-or-nothing treatment. You can't just try it out and decide after a minute or two. The patient was comatose and the family wanted him transferred to our inpatient hospice unit. But we couldn't accept him because we do not resuscitate our hospice patients on the unit. After I saw the patient's directive, I talked with the family and told them we were in a bind because not resuscitating the patient would be in direct conflict with his written wishes. The patient's son said, "Oh, I put that in, but I didn't know what it meant." We did eventually transfer the man to the inpatient unit, where he died very comfortably. I still feel funny about it, though, because of his written wishes.

Remember, it is important to write down only those treatment preferences that are legal in your state. No matter how adamant Dad might be on the subject, the directive is not the place to include "If it looks like I'm going to be a vegetable, please shoot me at sunset." Directives that contain illegal treatments or care preferences are considered null and void.

Also keep in mind that healthcare providers are not obligated to honor treatment preferences that are not medically reasonable. Mom might want to say, "I have a million dollar limit on my insurance policy. I want you to do everything medically possible within that limit. After that, I'll take comfort care." This statement would probably not be honored.

Organ Donation

If your parents are organ donors, they'll have to consider life support, at least temporarily. In order to keep a heart or kidney in optimal condition, life support is necessary until the organ can be removed.

Preferences about organ donation should be noted in the healthcare directive. You might consider language such as, "I am willing to be placed on a ventilator temporarily until my organs can be donated."

Comfort Care

As discussed earlier, people who do not want life-sustaining medical treatment will still want to be kept comfortable. Although pain control is the most obvious component of comfort care, comfort can mean many things. When filling out an advance directive, consider the following comfort measures:

- hospice care;
- pain control;
- relief of nausea, anxiety, shortness of breath, and other symptoms;
- assistance with daily baths and personal hygiene;
- in-home care; and
- massage, music, or other complementary therapies.

The Five Wishes directive includes a detailed list of statements about comfort measures. It also offers a number of phrases to help individuals indicate how they would like to be treated. For example, "I wish to have others by my side praying for me when possible," and "I wish to be cared for with kindness and cheerfulness, not sadness."

Designation of the Healthcare Agent

The healthcare agent will have a crucial role if ever your parents are unable to communicate for themselves. Your parents can designate one or more healthcare agents. Some people will name co-agents who must work together to follow the person's care wishes. Other people name a primary healthcare agent along with an alternate (or several alternates). The primary agent is the first person authorized to make decisions. If the primary agent is unavailable or unable to fulfill his or her responsibilities, an alternate agent can step in.

When filling out this part of the healthcare directive, the most important question to ask your parents is, "Who do you want to speak for you if you cannot speak for yourself?" The second most important question is, "If that person is unable to do the job, who else would you trust to speak for you?"

Naming the Agent

Most often, the person named as an agent is a family member—a spouse, child, or sibling. If your parents have an agent in mind, ask the following questions:

- Do you trust this person to carry out your wishes?
- Does this person have a clear understanding of your care wishes and goals?
- Is this person willing to accept the responsibilities of being a healthcare agent?
- Will this person be available to do the job?
- Does this person meet the legal requirements of a healthcare agent?

Trust. It's essential that your parents trust their agent. Whether or not you agree with their choice, remember that this is what your parents want. Even though you've never liked Aunt Harriet, Mom might have a close, trusting relationship with her. If she chooses Aunt Harriet as her healthcare agent, you will have to accept that decision. It is fair, however, to ask Aunt Harriet, "If it comes down to deciding Mom's care (hospice care, CPR, and so on), can we trust you to carry out Mom's wishes?"

When eighty-six-year-old Floyd named his son as his healthcare agent, he was happy to turn the decision making over to someone else. "My son knows what I want. It's a relief to let him worry about all that."

Understanding care wishes. The main purpose of a kitchen table discussion is to establish a common understanding of your parents' care wishes and goals. Once a healthcare agent is named, it's reasonable to ask him or her to reiterate what your parents want. It's crucial that the agent has a clear understanding of your parent's wishes—and the commitment to honor those wishes.

Melissa, a nurse in a small community hospital, tells of her frustrations with an elderly woman's healthcare agent:

The patient obviously hadn't had much of a discussion with her selected agent, who was a friend of hers. The agent insisted on doing things that the patient did not want to have done, as clearly stated in the healthcare directive. It really complicated matters. The agent did not agree with the patient's preferences—she was placing her own values above her friend's wishes. It put us in a terrible bind.

Accepting responsibility. Because the healthcare agent may have to act as a proxy for your parents, it's reasonable to ask, "Do you want to do this?" If your parents choose you to be their agent, and you don't feel you can do the job, be honest. "I can't be your agent, Dad. I have a hard time speaking up" or "I respect your right to make these choices, but I don't agree with them and it would be hard for me to carry them out."

Consider the story of Connie, a hospice nurse who was surprised to learn that a patient had named her as healthcare agent:

I was the hospice nurse for a woman in her late fifties who had a very advanced cancer. She was in a nursing home and her condition was changing quickly. On one visit, the patient was barely responsive. When I arrived for my next visit, the charge nurse summoned me. She pointed to the chart and said, "Look." The patient's healthcare directive had been inserted at the front of the chart. It was dated a week earlier and named me as her agent. I was flabbergasted. The patient had never talked with me about it. I wasn't sure it was even legal to put my name down, and I certainly was not comfortable making healthcare decisions for her.

Availability. Many families are scattered across the country, or even the world. If the named agent lives far away, he or she may find it difficult to perform the duties of an agent. In that situation, it's a good idea to name coagents, or at least an alternate agent who lives close by.

When Harry suddenly became ill and very confused, his only son, Dale, was out of the country. It took more than a day to finally reach him. Harry eventually recovered from his illness and was able to go home. Later, when Dale sat down with his father to discuss advance care planning and fill out a healthcare directive, they talked about the difficulties posed by Dale's travel schedule. Harry decided to keep Dale as his primary healthcare agent, but he also named his granddaughter, Mary, as an alternate agent in the event that Dale could not be reached.

If your parent's healthcare agent lives out of town, it's essential to keep that person informed. Also, make sure your parent's doctor knows that the healthcare agent lives far away.

Legal requirements. State laws vary on who can be appointed a healthcare agent. In some states, a healthcare provider—a doctor, nurse, or therapist, for example—cannot be appointed as agent unless that person is a relative. Make sure you understand the laws of the state where your parents reside.

Determining an Agent's Powers

Your parents can designate which powers they want to assign to their agent(s). For example, the Minnesota Health Care Directive is written with the following language, though individuals can alter this language to meet their needs:[1]

If I am unable to decide or speak for myself, my agent has the power to:

- *consent to, refuse, or withdraw my healthcare treatment, service, or procedure;*
- *stop or not start healthcare which is keeping or might keep me alive;*
- *choose my healthcare providers;*
- *choose where I live when I need healthcare and what personal security measures are needed to keep me safe; and*
- *obtain copies of my medical records and allow others to see them.*

Of course, your parents can also place limitations on their healthcare agent(s). For example:

- My healthcare agent does not have the power to move me to another state.
- I do not want my healthcare agent to make any financial decisions, including application for Medicare or Medicaid.

The healthcare agent is only responsible for healthcare decisions when Mom or Dad is unable to speak for herself or himself. If Mom suffers a stroke and is unable to make medical decisions, the healthcare agent can make them for her. If she recovers, the decision making goes back to Mom unless she specifically states that she wants the agent to continue making her medical decisions.

Changing Agents

Your parents' circumstances could change. If your father names your mother as his healthcare agent, and your mother dies or becomes incapacitated, your father will need to change the healthcare directive. Divorce can also affect the status of the healthcare agent. If your parents divorce, it would probably make sense for your parents to name new agents.

If your parents want to change agents for any reason, they will have to fill out a whole new healthcare directive. Be sure that your parents' family members and healthcare professionals are informed of the change.

Signatures

Remember, you do not need a lawyer to fill out a healthcare directive, nor do you need a lawyer to make it legal. Lawyers might have expertise in estate planning and drawing up wills, but that doesn't mean they understand healthcare options.

You will, however, need signatures to make the directive legal. How many and from whom depends on the state in which your parents live. In some states, you may need to have the document notarized.

Distribution

The healthcare directive isn't complete until copies are made and distributed. According to the U.S. Living Will Registry, 35 percent of healthcare directives cannot be found when needed.

Keep the original directive in an easily accessible place. Do not put it in a safety deposit box. In an emergency, you'll need to be able to quickly retrieve this document.

Kay remembers searching for her father's healthcare directive:

We were all scrambling around trying to find it for the nursing home, because we knew Dad had been very specific about not wanting to go back

into the hospital again. After days of searching, it turned up in his under-
wear drawer. We never figured out why he decided to keep it there.

When you distribute copies of the directive, it's a good idea to
note on each copy where the original is kept. Copies of the healthcare directive should be given to:

- the healthcare agent(s);
- doctors;
- other family members; and
- anyone else who's involved in your parents' healthcare.

Another good option to consider is a free service provided by
the U.S. Living Will Registry. The registry stores healthcare directives in a computer database, with each directive identified by a
social security number. When a hospital calls the registry to
request a copy of the document, the computer faxes a copy to the
hospital. (Privacy and confidentiality are strictly protected, as the
registry can only be accessed by hospitals.) With this service, you
do not need to inform the hospital that your document is on file.
The hospital will simply call the registry and, with your social
security number, check to see if your document is in the database.
(For more details about this service, see the appendix B.)

Will Paramedics Read the Healthcare Directive?

In most states, paramedics who are called to a medical emergency
will not read, much less try to interpret, a healthcare directive. If
your father's directive specifies that he does not want CPR, the
paramedics may still be obligated to perform resuscitation.

Mark describes his experience with the paramedics after finding
his mother dead in her home:

I found her on the floor. She was already cold. When I called 911 to report the death, they sent an ambulance. To my horror, the paramedics tried to perform CPR on her. I couldn't stop them.

Although paramedics will not read an advance directive, in most states they will honor a "do not resuscitate" (DNR) order—if it is kept in the home and signed by a physician (see page 47). In a handful of states (Arkansas, California, Indiana, Kansas, Maryland, Nevada, New Mexico, and Wisconsin), emergency response teams will also recognize MedicAlert bracelets engraved with "DNR" as a valid DNR order.

The seven states that do not honor DNRs outside an institutional setting are Delaware, Iowa, Mississippi, Nebraska, North Dakota, Pennsylvania, and Vermont.

The Role of the Healthcare Agent

Suppose you become the healthcare agent for your parents. Consider this an honor. It means that your parents have faith in you and trust you to speak for them. Yes, it is a lot of work, but it also can yield a great reward: knowing that you will be the one to ensure that your parents' wishes are honored. As a woman who was the agent for both her mother-in-law and father-in-law said, "I was overwhelmed that they loved me enough to place such faith and trust in me. That faith and trust kept me going through some very tough decisions."

As healthcare agent, you must be prepared to play several roles: spokesperson, advocate, and reviewer.

Spokesperson

As any doctor or nurse will tell you, it's essential to have one contact person during a medical crisis. This way, healthcare professionals can convey accurate and up-to-date information to the family. As the spokesperson for your parents, you will become "information central." This means that all information will be directed at you.

Make sure that everyone, including your family and all the healthcare workers, understands that you are the spokesperson. This is particularly important in a hospital setting. Otherwise, with the rapid pace of medical decisions, the person at the bedside may be the one who is given crucial information and asked to make decisions.

Anne, who was the healthcare agent for her father, tells of her experience as spokesperson:

Fortunately, because I am a nurse and because I'm the one who talked with Dad about his healthcare directive, everyone in the family looked to me for decision making. I knew Dad did not want any kind of feeding tube. Wouldn't you know that one afternoon, while I was at work, a doctor (who did not know my dad) stopped in and said they were going to insert a "temporary" tube because he couldn't swallow. He didn't even ask whether this was okay. I got a panicked call from my niece, saying, "What should we do? Grandpa is too confused to make a decision." I had to call the doctor and the hospital and say, "Wait. We need to talk about this." I shudder to think what would have happened if my niece hadn't been on the scene.

Advocate

Often, care decisions need to be made during times of high emotional stress. Healthcare systems and hospitals are not always "friendly" to the wishes of patients, family members, or healthcare agents. Moreover, families can be torn apart by a medical crisis or disagreement over a loved one's care. As the healthcare agent, it will be your responsibility to advocate for your parent's wishes. Be warned: you might run into some controversy.

Anne continues her story:

I gathered the family together—Mom, my brothers and sisters, and my children, nieces, and nephews—to explain Dad's decision about the feeding tube. I said, "The doctor says Dad can't swallow anymore. He wants to put a tube down Dad's nose into his stomach for a couple of weeks to see if the swallowing will get better. If we don't do this, he will probably die in a week to ten days." Mom spoke up quickly: "He wouldn't want that tube." So we told the hospital staff: no tube. The next day, I was accosted by Dad's day nurse. "Why aren't you going to help him?" she demanded. If Dad hadn't been so clear in his wishes, I might have backed down right then and there.

Anne experienced a rollercoaster of guilt and second thoughts about the feeding tube:

I knew this is what Dad wanted, but somehow I felt like his executioner. I had to keep stepping back to tell myself that, first of all, this was Dad's decision, and second of all, I didn't cause his system to shut down like it did. I didn't realize how hard all this would be, but I'm glad I kept my promise and honored his wishes.

If you are your parents' healthcare agent, you may one day feel burdened with the responsibility of upholding their wishes. It's important to remember that these are not your choices, but your parents'. Your charge is to honor their decisions.

The fact that your parents have designated an agent means they have considered their care ahead of time. When Sandy's mother had a severe stroke, the doctor set up a family conference to discuss care options. "I was afraid he was going to give us a whole bunch of options to choose from," she recalls. "Instead, the doctor sat down with Mom's living will in front of him. He said, 'You are so lucky that she made the way so clear for you.'"

Reviewer

As your parents' healthcare agent, be prepared to review their care choices from time to time. Treatment choices often change as a person's health changes. When Dad was diagnosed with cancer, he may have declared "no artificial hydration" on his healthcare directive. After recovering from chemotherapy, however, he might have changed his mind.

As the healthcare agent for his incapacitated mother, Dan had second thoughts after deciding against a feeding tube:

We'd written up the living will over five years ago. Mom had been specific about not wanting a feeding tube, but I always meant to discuss it with her again. I never got around to it. When it came to making the decision, we chose not to have the tube put in. I had this little voice in the back of my head saying, "Are you sure this is what she wants?" She died peacefully, but I still regret that we never talked about it again.

You Are Not the Lone Ranger

If you feel overwhelmed with responsibility, rest assured, you do not have to bear it alone. You can ask for help. If Mom is suffering a healthcare crisis or is dying, you may need the support of family, friends, healthcare staff, and perhaps clergy.

Talk with the nurse who is caring for your parent. Ask for a family conference with the doctor and the social worker. Involve the hospital chaplain if you think he or she can help. Also, almost every hospital has a patient representative or an ethics committee available.

The Other Kind of Will

When filling out a healthcare directive, don't be surprised if your parents want to talk about their wills. This can be a very touchy subject. As Kathleen Adams, a reporter for *Time* magazine wrote, "How do you ruin a perfectly good relationship with your parents? Ask them, ahem, about the will."[2]

If your parents want to talk about their will or their finances, don't discourage them. You should never turn down an opportunity to gather information from your parents. Instead, ask the following questions, and be sure to take notes. The information you gain could be invaluable in a crisis.

- Do you have a written will or trust? If so, where is it kept?
- Do you have an attorney who has worked with you on financial issues?
- Do you have a durable power of attorney—someone who has access to your bank accounts in case you become incapacitated?
- Who knows where to find important documents such as insurance policies, birth certificates, bank account information, and investment information?

If your parents want to talk about financial issues, *A Family Caregiver's Guide to Planning and Decision Making for the Elderly*, by James A. Wilkinson, contains excellent checklists and practical advice on finances and financial planning.

Congratulations!

If you succeed in helping your parents complete a healthcare directive, you can feel very proud of your kitchen table discussion. Less than 25 percent of people in the United States actually have a written document. But before sending everyone home, make a date to sit down at the table again in three months, six months, or a year. As we've stated before, care wishes and goals can change.

Now, relax and enjoy the coffee.

REFERENCES

1. M. Stum, PhD, "The Minnesota Health Care Directive," University of Minnesota Extension Service, August 1998. Used with permission. To order this document, call the Minnesota Board on Aging's Senior Linkage Line at 1-800-333-2433.
2. K. Adams, "Balancing Tack and Tactics," *Time* magazine, May 15, 2000.

9

Understanding Hospice Care

I don't want to achieve immortality through my work . . .
I want to achieve it through not dying.
Woody Allen

Perhaps you are having a kitchen table discussion because one of your parents is dying. The elephant in the living room is bursting through the walls, and you need to know what options are available. Now is the time to seriously explore hospice care.

When we talk about hospice, we are getting into the most difficult part of a kitchen table discussion. Hospice is a care choice for people who are dying. As one son put it, "It seems to me when you bring up the word 'hospice,' you are saying that my dad has received a death sentence." How do you get beyond the phrase "death sentence" to understanding what hospice is all about?

This section provides a very basic overview of hospice care, but several excellent books are available that go into much greater depth. You may also want to contact your local hospice program, your state hospice organization, or the National Hospice and Palliative Care Organization for further information. (See appendix B.)

What Is Hospice?

First, hospice is not a building or a place, but a special kind of care for people who are dying. The focus of hospice is to ensure that a person's remaining days are comfortable. It is considered the gold standard of care for people at the end of life's journey. Hospice care:

- emphasizes living as fully as possible;
- relieves the physical, emotional, and spiritual distress that often accompany a life-limiting illness;
- supports the family while they are caring for their loved one; and
- provides grief support after the death.

Most hospice patients are able to spend their final days in the comfort of their own home. For those who cannot be at home, hospice care is provided in a hospital, nursing home, or residential setting.

How Does It Work?

Suppose Dad is in the hospital with serious breathing problems caused by a chronic lung disease. On top of that, his diabetes is causing serious circulation problems, and he has just been diagnosed with prostate cancer. His doctor has been forthright: "In general, things are falling apart. We don't have any miracle treatment here. I would be surprised if your father lived more than six months. It's time to think about hospice care."

Dad's doctor would make a referral to a hospice program. Most likely, a hospice nurse or social worker would visit you and your father in the hospital to explain the benefits of hospice and help determine the best place of care. If Dad cannot be cared for at home, he can receive hospice care in a nursing home, assisted living facility, or hospice residence (a homelike residence used exclusively for hospice patients). If he was going to be cared for at home, the hospice staff would arrange for the necessary medical equipment, such as oxygen or a hospital bed, before he was discharged from the hospital.

After discharge, the hospice program would tailor Dad's care according to his and the family's needs. This might include an aide to help with bathing, a volunteer to provide companionship or a break for the family, and regular nurse visits. Your family would have access to a twenty-four-hour call service if any problems were to arise.

If Dad required hospitalization at some point, hospice personnel would not only arrange for it, they would continue to care for him during his hospital stay. In addition, if the family needed a break from caregiving, hospice would provide respite care.

How Do We Arrange for Hospice Care?

First, talk with your parent's doctor. Hospice programs must have a physician's order to provide services. To receive hospice care:

- The patient must have a prognosis of six months or less, as certified by a physician.
- The patient must sign a consent form agreeing to comfort care rather than curative or life-prolonging treatment.

Look for a hospice program that is Medicare certified. Medicare certification not only allows the program to bill Medicare for services, it also assures that the program meets rigorous Medicare standards for care. If you have several hospice programs in your area, talk with your parent's physician. He or she has probably worked with one or more of these programs. You can also ask your parent's clinic, home care nurse, or hospital social worker for help in choosing a hospice program, or contact the National Hospice and Palliative Care Organization for a nationwide listing of programs.

Who Pays for Hospice Care?

Hospice is covered by Medicare, Medicaid, and most private insurance companies. The Medicare hospice benefit includes:

- medical and symptom management focused on enhancing comfort (care is provided by a team of professionals, including the patient's primary physician, nurses, and the hospice medical director);
- emotional and spiritual care, including visits by social workers and chaplains;
- medical supplies, medical equipment, and medications related to the terminal diagnosis;
- assistance with bathing, personal care, and homemaking;
- hospitalization or extended hours of home care for acute episodes;
- volunteers to provide companionship and run errands;
- respite care when the family is exhausted or unable to provide care; and
- grief support both before and after the death.

Please note: Hospice benefits do not pay for curative or life-prolonging treatments and procedures. If Dad wants to go to Mexico for the latest cure he read about on the Web, hospice is probably not the program for him.

If you have specific questions about coverage, call your local hospice program to inquire about the Medicare hospice benefit.

Discussing Hospice with Mom and Dad

Many people hesitate to bring up the subject of hospice care. Common fears and questions include:

- How do I know this is the right time to talk about it? What if Mom isn't dying?
- If I talk about this with Dad, he might give up hope.
- What if I bring it up and Mom says no?
- Does hospice mean that the doctors will quit treating Dad's illness?

If you are considering a hospice discussion, trust your instincts. Predicting a six-month prognosis is difficult even for professionals. If you think the time is right, it probably is. Also trust your parents' instincts. If their bodies are failing, they may know better than anyone when death is approaching.

Rebecca, a seasoned hospice nurse, was unable to predict how much time her own mother had left.

I knew things were changing with her, but I was so wrapped up in the day-to-day care that I didn't put it all together. In retrospect, I should have worked harder at getting Mom enrolled in hospice at the beginning of the summer. It would have been so much easier for Dad, and for the rest of us. As it was, she had hospice care for the last two weeks of her life. It was wonderful, but we could have used the help much sooner.

What If Mom Isn't Dying?

If you are wondering whether it's time for hospice, ask your parents for permission to talk with their doctor. Explain to the doctor why you are concerned. He or she might see Mom on a regular basis, but may not know that Mom is now having difficulty walking from the bedroom to the living room. Ask specific questions, "Would you be surprised if Mom were still with us in six months? In a year?" If the answer is yes, it's time to consider hospice.

I Don't Want Dad to Give Up Hope

Suppose you are sitting at the kitchen table watching your father pick at his sweet roll. You know he's not doing well—his doctor has been straightforward about it—yet, when you open your mouth to say "hospice," nothing comes out. A little voice in the back of your head says, "Don't bring it up. He'll lose all hope and give up."

When the words won't come, keep in mind the following. First, hope has many different meanings. Second, it's usually not the person who gives up; it's the body that wears out.

For people who recognize and understand that life is drawing to a close, hope can take on a whole new dimension. Instead of hoping for a longer life or for a cure, they may hope for:

- the opportunity to take care of unfinished business;
- enough time to say goodbye; and
- to live their last days and weeks in comfort.

A young mother with advanced breast cancer used her time to write letters for her children to read at each birthday until they turned eighteen. The hospice social worker said, "Once she knew that she didn't have to exhaust herself with treatments, she could turn her attention to her children. She left them an incredible gift."

What If Mom Says No?

Sometimes you need to lay the groundwork and give it time. It may be helpful to say, "I'm bringing up hospice because I think it can help you to be more comfortable. The hospice staff can help the rest of us take care of you."

Always remember your table manners. You might think it's time for hospice, and the doctor might think it's time for hospice, but this is Mom's decision. If she says, "No, I don't want that," respect her right to choose.

Will the Doctors Quit Treating Dad's Illness?

This is one of the most common fears about hospice—that patients will be abandoned by their doctors and will not receive treatment when they need it. Doctors are certainly guilty of perpetuating this fear when they say, "There's nothing more I can do for you. I'm going to refer you to hospice." But "nothing more" usually means "nothing to cure your disease or prolong your life."

Even when a disease cannot be cured, a lot can be done at the end of life. Hospice professionals are experts in palliative care (treatment that focuses on comfort and the relief of symptoms). When symptoms are relieved, quality of life often improves.

Jill's quality of life changed for the better after she enrolled in hospice:

Now that I'm in hospice, I don't worry about pain anymore. Sure, I have it, but I know that people will believe me when I say I hurt and they will work to make it better. Before hospice, nurses would say to me, "Oh, pain is normal with your condition." I was in constant fear of it.

Moreover, hospice patients are usually able to keep their regular physician. Most likely, Dad's doctor will continue to direct his care, and hospice nurses will keep in close contact with the doctor.

Suggestions for Discussing Hospice Care

Because hospice can be such a difficult topic for both you and your parents, its discussion deserves specific guidelines:

- **Find out as much as you can about hospice before coming to the table.**
- **Understand your parent's perspective on hospice.** Rather than say, "Mom, it's clear you're going to die soon. Let's talk hospice," try, "I'm concerned about your comfort. What do you know about hospice? Can we talk about it?"
- **Be prepared for some tough questions:** "Does hospice mean I'm dying?" "Are you trying to send me someplace?" "What about my doctor?" Seek help from hospice workers. They will be able to answer some of your questions.

A discussion about hospice care may be the greatest gift you can give to your parents—and the greatest gift they can give to you. As Dame Cicely Saunders, founder of the modern hospice movement said, "You matter to the last moment of your life, and we will do all we can, not only to help you die peacefully, but to live until you die."

10

Kitchen Table Calamities

I have yet to see any problem, however complicated,
which, when you looked at it in the right way,
did not become still more complicated.

Poul Anderson

Most kitchen tables have been the setting for some kind of mishap. At one time or another, someone spills the milk or drops the antique gravy boat that's been in the family for generations. Just as we expect a certain amount of calamity at the kitchen table, we can expect problems to arise before, during, and after a kitchen table discussion. For example:

> • You try to initiate a kitchen table discussion, but your parents simply won't talk.

- A parent has a healthcare crisis before you've had your kitchen table discussion.
- You disagree with a parent's care choices.
- In a medical emergency, treatments are started that your parent did not want.
- The healthcare facility refuses to honor your parent's healthcare directive.
- The healthcare agent is not supporting your parent's wishes.
- You and your family cannot agree on the treatments your parent should receive.

Mom and Dad Won't Talk

Suppose you've gathered everyone at the table, good intentions and a healthcare directive in hand, and your parents refuse to talk. You try all the opening phrases, all the little tips to get the conversation going, but Mom looks at her coffee cup and says, "I don't want to talk about it." Now what?

Don't give up. It might take time for this conversation to happen. It might take a crisis. Or it might take something as simple as filling out your own healthcare directive first.

Irene talks about the first healthcare discussion she had with her mother:

She started to cry when I brought it up. She was sure I knew something about her health that I wasn't telling her. I finally got her to settle down when I said, "You know, I've filled out my own living will." She looked at me, surprised. "You have?" she asked. "Yes," I said. "If something should happen to me, I don't want my husband stuck with all the decision making."

If your best efforts fail and you cannot get this conversation going, ask your parents, "Mom and Dad, are you aware of the default?"

The default is what happens when no other options are chosen. In our healthcare system, the default generally means tests, treatments, surgery, and other aggressive efforts focused on saving the person's life. Most healthcare professionals have a story or two about the default, ranging from the case of a frail, bed-ridden ninety-year-old who was put through cardiac surgery, only to die five days later in intensive care, to the case of a nursing home that called the paramedics to resuscitate a woman who had just died from cancer.

We need to emphasize that this discussion still belongs to your parents. Mom may have rational (or irrational) reasons for not having this conversation. She has the right to say, "I don't want to talk about it." A decision to make no decision is still a decision. As W. C. Fields once said, "If at first you don't succeed, try, try, and try again. Then give up. There's no sense being a darn fool about it."

But We Haven't Gotten to the Kitchen Table Yet!

What if you have to make a crucial decision about your parent's healthcare, but you haven't had the care planning discussion?

Consider this scenario: Your father is an eighty-year-old widower who has suffered from congestive heart failure for several years. He is still independent, but he's become very forgetful. You've never talked with him about a healthcare directive or about his care wishes. One day you get a call from the building caretaker: Your father has been found unconscious on the floor. By the time you reach the emergency room, his breathing is so bad they've put him on a ventilator. Twenty-four hours later, a doctor comes to you and says, "It looks like his bowel is obstructed. We need permission to operate. If we don't, he probably won't live very long. And if we do, I can't guarantee that he will come out of this."

Now what do you do?

This is the time to gather the family and have a kitchen table discussion—without your father. You can still put together information about his goals, preferences, fears, and experiences. You may find that somewhere, sometime, Dad has talked about these things. He might have said, "Boy, my friend Bill had a tough time of it. I sure wouldn't want to end up in a nursing home like he did." Or, "I grew up in this house, and I want to die in this house."

Next, have a frank conversation with the doctor. Sacramento Health Care Decisions has put together an excellent booklet, *Finding Your Way,* that can help you ask the right questions:[1]

- Is it still possible to cure this illness?
- If no cure is possible, what are the chances that Dad will improve? Will he regain his independence?
- Given Dad's current condition, what do you see in the next few days, weeks, months?
- What other options are available?
- Is comfort care the best choice?

It's also reasonable to ask, "Given the circumstances and Dad's overall condition, what do you recommend?" Then, based on the doctor's assessment and on what you know about your father's values, you may be able to reach a decision.

Jill and her mother had never really talked about advance care planning. After her mother had a severe stroke, Jill consulted with the neurologist before making a decision about treatment:

It was hard to have this conversation because Mom was so independent up until the stroke. The neurologist was very honest. I appreciated it when he said, "In a stroke this severe, the best I can see down the road is a minimal return to any kind of independence. If you decide to place the feeding tube, she will need to be in a nursing home for the rest of her life." I knew Mom well enough to know that she wouldn't want it. I said, "No feeding tube." Instead, we enrolled her in hospice care and brought her home with us. It was still very hard, but I kept picturing her alone in a nursing home, being cared for by strangers. That wasn't Mom.

I Don't Agree with My Parents' Care Choices

What if you're sitting at the kitchen table, talking with Dad about his healthcare wishes, when he makes a decision that you totally disagree with? For example, Jerry's eighty-six-year-old father announced, "I'm going to quit taking all my pills. I don't see any sense in it anymore." He felt that his quality of life had so diminished that there was no reason to extend his life. Jerry, on the other hand, enjoyed spending time with his father and felt that quality of life remained.

"But Dad, you can't do that," Jerry said.

"Why not?" his father replied. "It's my life and I'm tired of it."

Jerry felt that his father was making a foolish decision that could result in serious health consequences and perhaps a shortened life. When disagreements like this arise, it's sometimes helpful to take a systematic approach.

- **First, ask yourself why you disagree with the decision.** Are you thinking about your parent's well-being, or your own? Are you and your parent having a clash of values or beliefs?
- **Find out the reasons behind your parent's decision.** Ask, "Why have you decided to do this?" The answer may be straightforward: "I can't afford to buy the pills anymore." It may be complex: "I don't feel my life has meaning anymore."

- **Negotiate.** Jerry said, "Dad, I know things are hard for you a lot of the time, but the pills are keeping you from becoming sicker. Why don't you stay on them until your next doctor's appointment and we'll discuss it with her?"
- **If you can't negotiate an agreement, ask for outside help.** You might have to say, "Dad, I'd like to call your doctor and see what she says about the medications."
- **Be aware that not all disagreements can be worked out.** Ultimately, the decisions belong to your parents, not to you.

But Mom Didn't Want That Treatment!

Suppose you've had your kitchen table discussion. Mom has written down her wishes and appointed you as her agent. Then one day, Mom falls and breaks her hip. Later, during surgery, her heart stops. She is resuscitated and is now on a ventilator in the intensive care unit. All of this happened so quickly that you didn't have time to discuss it with the doctors. Mom had stated in her directive that she did not want to be placed on a ventilator. When you tell this to the doctor, he says, "It was necessary. We want to leave it on for a few days to see if she can breathe on her own."

Now what? First, remember that treatment decisions sometimes need to be made quickly. There may have been no time to consult the healthcare directive or agent. Second, if the doctor knew your mother's wishes, the decision to place her on a ventilator may have fallen into the gray zone. Although the healthcare directive said "no ventilator," short-term use might make sense if there's a reasonable chance she'll recover and return to her former state of health.

Now the question is, should you continue the treatment? In a case like this, it's important to communicate with the doctors and other healthcare professionals. Take the following steps:

- **Find a copy of the healthcare directive specifying Mom's wishes and naming the healthcare agent.**
- **Ask a nurse, social worker, or chaplain to help you pull together a conference with your family and the doctors in charge of your mother's care.**
- **Review the directive at the conference.** Be prepared to ask questions about chances of improvement, quality of life, and what you might expect in the next days, weeks, or months. Ask the doctors, "Does it make sense to continue this treatment?"
- **Once you have all the information, if you believe that the treatment is against Mom's wishes, ask to have the treatment discontinued.** If you are having trouble coming to a decision, ask for help. Most hospitals have an ethics committee that is trained to help families deal with difficult decisions.

What Do You Mean, You Won't Honor the Directive?

You may find that hospitals, nursing homes, and other institutions have policies that conflict with your parents' care wishes. Consider this story related by Chris, a hospice coordinator:

I was called by a very distraught man named Thomas. His mother, Vivian, had advanced Alzheimer's, and the nursing home was tying her arms down and forcing food into her. "Several years ago," he said, "when she was still clear, Mom said that she did not want to be force-fed. But the nursing home won't stop. They say it's against their policy not to feed a patient. The doctor is no help, either. She says that if we didn't feed her, we would be killing her. I just want them to stop tying her hands. If she pushes the food away, let her."

After some discussion with the nursing home administrator and the doctor, I understood that they would not change the way they were treating Vivian. I helped Thomas arrange for a transfer to another doctor and a nursing home that would honor her wishes. We then enrolled her in hospice. The hospice program supported the nursing home staff through the difficult time of allowing Vivian to refuse food. She died peacefully about three months later.

From the start, it's important to establish a clear understanding with the nursing home, hospital, or doctor about your parent's care wishes. In most states, physicians and healthcare facilities who conscientiously object to a healthcare directive may legally refuse to honor it. However, this must be discussed up front, upon admission, and the staff must help the patient transfer to another doctor or facility if the patient or agent requests it.[2] If your parents' directive is not going to be honored, seek another facility or another doctor.

The Healthcare Agent Is Not Supporting Your Parent's Wishes

Suppose Mom names your stepfather, Ralph, as her healthcare agent. She is in the late stages of heart failure and has told you that if her heart stops she does not want to be resuscitated under any circumstances. In a private conversation, Ralph tells you, "But I love her so much. I'll try anything to keep her with me a little longer."

If you have the luxury of knowing in advance that the agent does not want to carry out Mom's wishes, it's time to gather everyone at the kitchen table and say, "We need to talk." It's also time to make sure that Mom puts her wishes in writing.

Unfortunately, this situation is more likely to come up when Mom is no longer able to communicate. If the healthcare directive does not give specific instructions other than "I trust Ralph to make decisions for me," it's important to talk to Ralph. This kind of discussion is best facilitated by a neutral person, preferably a social worker or chaplain. If you cannot resolve your differences, consider asking for help from the facility's ethics committee.

Except in the case of moral objection, doctors and healthcare providers are legally bound to honor a written healthcare directive. If the directive specifically states a wish that the agent is not supporting, ask for help from the doctor.

The Family Can't Agree on Dad's Treatment

Even the best-prepared healthcare directive cannot address all the treatment decisions that may come up. Let's say that Dad has developed severe complications after heart surgery. He is currently in a coma, receiving fluids and medications through an IV. The doctor has brought up the possibility of stopping the IV because it's causing fluids to build up in Dad's lungs.

Over the years, Dad has made it clear that he does not want extraordinary measures to keep him alive. His healthcare directive states that in the case of a terminal condition, he wants comfort measures only.

You believe that Dad's condition is terminal and that the IV fluids are contributing to his discomfort. Therefore, you feel that the IV goes against his wishes and should be discontinued. Your mother, brother, and sister, however, aren't convinced that he's terminal. They want the treatment continued. Clearly, it's time for another kitchen table discussion.

The decision to continue or withdraw treatment may not be as black and white as it appears. What has Dad said in the past about his preferences, goals, values, and experiences? Have you talked with the doctor about outcomes, risks, and benefits? You may want to ask someone outside the family, such as the hospital social worker or chaplain, to facilitate this conversation.

Bill, a doctor, talks about his experience with his father-in-law, Harold:

Short of a miracle, I knew that Harold wasn't going to live—with or without the IV fluids and medications. I could see that the fluid was increasing his congestion and making his breathing uncomfortable. In fact, a nurse had to come in several times a day to suction him. The rest of the family was clinging to the hope that somehow the IV would buy time for a miracle. No one could agree on what to do, and emotions were running high.

Eventually we compromised. Every day I asked for the IV to be turned down a little more. After the third day, the family was ready to stop it altogether—as long as it could be restarted if they changed their minds. I asked the nurse to keep the IV in place with only enough fluid to keep it open. Harold died two days later. By then, everyone had come to grips with the situation.

Troubleshooting

If you are in the midst of a kitchen table calamity, here are a few tips:

- **Call a family conference and make sure all key decision makers are invited.**
- **Ask health professionals for their expert opinions.**
- **Give yourself and your family time to work through the decision.**
- **Above all, keep the conversation focused on your parents.** This is about what they want. In order to honor your parents' wishes, you may have to make a difficult or

unpopular decision. Remember, you are doing this out of love and respect.

- **If a healthcare directive exists, remember that it's a legal document.** You may have to call an attorney to make sure your parents' wishes are honored.

References

1. Adapted from *Finding Your Way: A Guide for End of Life Medical Decisions* (Carmichael, Calif.: Sacramento Health Care Decisions, 1999).

2. C. P. Sabatino, *"10 Legal Myths about Advance Medical Directives"* (American Bar Association, Commission on Legal Problems for the Elderly, Washington D.C.), http://www.abanet.org/elderly/myths.html, accessed March 2001.

APPENDIX A: STATE LAWS ON HEALTHCARE DIRECTIVES

Healthcare directives and healthcare agent designations must be completed in accordance with individual state law. Below is a list of states that recognize healthcare directives, healthcare agents, and DNR orders (outside of the hospital). For instance, the state of Alaska will recognize a healthcare directive, but will not recognize a healthcare agent. Delaware does not allow a non-hospital DNR order.

Because laws change frequently, it's a good idea to consult your state Area Agency on Aging for specific details about the laws in your state.

	Recognizes Healthcare Directive	Recognizes Healthcare Agent	Recognizes Non-hospital DNR Orders
Alabama	•	•	•
Alaska	•		•
Arizona	•	•	•
Arkansas	•	•	•
California	•	•	•
Colorado	•	•	•
Connecticut	•	•	•
Delaware	•	•	
District of Columbia	•	•	•
Florida	•	•	•
Georgia	•	•	•

	Recognizes Healthcare Directive	Recognizes Healthcare Agent	Recognizes Non-hospital DNR Orders
Hawaii	•	•	•
Idaho	•	•	•
Illinois	•	•	•
Indiana	•	•	•
Iowa	•	•	
Kansas	•	•	•
Kentucky	•	•	•
Louisiana	•	•	•
Maine	•	•	•
Maryland	•	•	•
Massachusetts	•		•
Michigan	•		•
Minnesota	•	•	•
Mississippi	•	•	
Missouri	•	•	•
Montana	•	•	•
Nebraska	•	•	
Nevada	•	•	•
New Hampshire	•	•	•
New Jersey	•	•	•
New Mexico	•	•	•
New York	•		•
North Carolina	•	•	•
North Dakota	•	•	
Ohio	•	•	•
Oklahoma	•	•	•

	Recognizes Healthcare Directive	Recognizes Healthcare Agent	Recognizes Non-hospital DNR Orders
Oregon	•	•	•
Pennsylvania	•	•	
Rhode Island	•	•	•
South Carolina	•	•	•
South Dakota	•	•	•
Tennessee	•	•	•
Texas	•	•	•
Utah	•	•	•
Vermont	•	•	
Virginia	•	•	•
Washington	•	•	•
West Virginia	•	•	•
Wisconsin	•	•	•
Wyoming	•	•	•

Advance Directives

Agencies, Organizations, and Web Sites

Aging with Dignity

P.O. Box 1661

Tallahassee, FL 32302-1661

888-5-WISHES

850-681-2010

Web site: www.agingwithdignity.org

E-mail: fivewishes@aol.com

For a small fee, this organization provides an on-line copy of "Five Wishes," a healthcare directive that is legal in thirty-six states.

MedicAlert Foundation

P.O. Box 381009

Turlock, CA 95382

800-432-5378

888-633-4298

Web site: www.medicalert.com

Provides bracelets containing personal medical information, including a DNR emblem that is recognized as a valid DNR order in Arkansas, California, Indiana, Kansas, Maryland, Nevada, New Mexico, and Wisconsin. Will also store a copy of a healthcare directive that can be retrieved when necessary, twenty-four hours a day.

The Medical Directive
P.O. Box 6100
Holliston, MA 01746-6100
800-214-4553
Web site: www.medicaldirective.org

Offers end-of-life care worksheets to help people determine the treatment they would want if ever they became gravely ill and unable to speak for themselves.

Midwest Bioethics Center
1021–1025 Jefferson Street
Kansas City, MO 64105
800-344-3829
Web site: www.midbio.org
E-mail: bioethic@midbio.org

Offers a program called "Caring Conversations: Making Your Wishes Known for End-of-Life Care," which provides a workbook on end-of-life issues, a consumer education booklet on healthcare and end-of-life decisions, a study guide and video, and other information.

Partnership for Caring (formerly Choices in Dying)
1620 Eye Street N.W., Suite 202
Washington, DC 20007
800-989-WILL (9455)
Web site: www.partnershipforcaring.org

Provides a twenty-four-hour hotline for up-to-date information about advance directive laws in individual states, as well as general information about end-of-life issues and decision making. Also provides advance directives for individual states.

U.S. Living Will Registry

P.O. Box 2789

523 Westfield Avenue

Westfield, NJ 07091-2789

800-LIV-WILL (548-9455)

Web site: www.livingwillregistry.com

E-mail: admin@uslivingwillregistry.com

A free nationwide service that registers and stores advance directives on a computer database and then faxes them directly to hospitals upon request.

Books and Publications

Baines, Barry. *The Ethical Will Resource Kit.* Minneapolis: Josaba Ltd., 1999. (Also available at www.ethicalwill.com.)

Wilkinson, James A. *A Family Caregiver's Guide to Planning and Decision Making for the Elderly.* Minneapolis: Fairview Press, 1999.

Assistance for Seniors/Elder Support Networks

Agencies, Organizations, and Web Sites

American Association of Retired Persons (AARP)
601 E Street N.W.
Washington, DC 20049
800-424-3410
Web site: www.aarp.org

Provides comprehensive information and services for seniors, including on-line support groups and various publications pertinent to older adults.

American Society on Aging (ASA)
833 Market Street, Suite 511
San Francisco, CA 94103
800-537-9728
415-974-0300
Web site: www.asaging.org
E-mail: info@asaging.org

A professional society that provides educational programs, publications, and training resources about a variety of topics on aging, such as multicultural issues, mental health, business and finance, healthcare, and spirituality.

Association of Jewish Family and Children's Agencies
557 Cranbury Road, Suite 2
East Brunswick, NJ 08816
800-634-7346

A referral service to the closest Jewish family service organization in your area. These agencies provide elder support.

Eldercare Locator
330 Independence Avenue, S.W.
Washington, DC 20201
800-677-1116
Web site: www.aoa.dhhs.gov/elderpage/locator.html

A free nationwide directory to help older persons and caregivers locate local support services and contact their state Area Agency on Aging. It is a public service of the Administration on Aging and the U.S. Department of Health and Human Services, administered by the National Association of Area Agencies on Aging and the National Association of State Units on Aging.

First Call for Help
United Way of America
701 North Fairfax Street
Alexandria, VA 22314-2045
703-836-7100
Web site: www.unitedway.org

The United Way of America provides support for human services programs, including elderly services, throughout the country. To contact your local United Way office, enter your zip code at the United Way web site, or check your local directory.

National Aging Information Center (NAIC)

330 Independence Avenue S.W., Room 4656

Washington, DC 20201

202-619-7501

Web site: www.aoa.dhhs.gov/NAIC/default.htm

E-mail: naic@aoa

NAIC provides a wide variety of information for older people, their families, and those who assist older persons. NAIC resources include program- and policy-related materials for consumers and practitioners, as well as demographic and other statistical data on the health, economic, and social conditions of older Americans.

National Association of Area Agencies on Aging

1112 16th Street N.W., Suite 100

Washington, DC 20036-4823

202-296-8130

Provides contact information for state Area Agencies on Aging.

National Institute on Aging (NIA)

Building 31, Room 5C27

31 Center Drive, MSC 2292

Bethesda, MD 20892

301-496-1752

800-222-2225

TTY: 800-222-4225

Web site: www.nih.gov/nia/

Offers a wide variety of free publications for the general public, including booklets about exercise, menopause, and dietary supplements. Also offers information for health professionals about cardiovascular health, aging, and effective clinician/patient communication.

Resource Directory for Older People

202-512-1800

Web site: www.aoa.dhhs.gov/aoa/dir/intro.html

The Resource Directory for Older People is a cooperative effort of the National Institute on Aging (NIA) and the Administration on Aging (AoA). It serves a wide audience including older people and their families, health and legal professionals, social service providers, librarians, researchers, and others with an interest in the field of aging. This on-line directory contains contact information for Federal Government agencies, AoA-supported resource centers, professional societies, private groups, and volunteer programs. Inclusion in the directory does not imply an endorsement or recommendation by NIA or AoA.

To receive a printed version of this directory (publication number 0106200145-6), write to Superintendent of Documents, P.O. Box 371954, Pittsburgh, PA 15250-7954.

Senior Scape Elderlinks

Web site: www.seniorscape.com

An on-line, up-to-date list of eldercare resources.

Assistance for Family Caregivers

Agencies, Organizations, and Web Sites

Caregivers Survival Resources
c/o Pathway Books
P.O. Box 27790
Golden Valley, MN 55427-0790
763-553-9783
800-958-3375, access code 32
Web site: www.caregiver911.com

Provides information about health-related agencies and general resources for caregivers.

CareGuide
739 Bryant Street
San Francisco, CA 94107
800-777-3319
415-474-1278
Fax: 415-474-1353
E-mail: care@careguide.com

CareGuide offers care management services and contact information for nursing homes, retirement communities, elderlaw attorneys, adult daycare centers, in-home medical services, respite care, assisted living centers, state and county senior agencies, and more. CareGuide also publishes information sheets on various topics. There are fees charged for many of the services.

National Family Caregivers Association

10400 Connecticut Avenue, #500

Kensington, MD 20895-3944

800-896-3650

Fax: 301-942-2302

Web site: www.nfcacares.org

E-mail: info@nfcacares

Provides education and advocacy for family caregivers.

National Federation of Interfaith Volunteer Caregivers

One West Armour Boulevard, Suite 202

Kansas City, MO 64111

816-931-5442

Fax: 816-931-5202

Web site: www.nfivc.org

E-mail: info@interfaithcaregivers.org

Locates volunteers to support the frail elderly and their caregivers.

The Well Spouse Foundation

30 East 40th Street PH

New York, NY 10016

212-685-8815

800-838-0879

Fax: 212-685-8676

Web site: www.wellspouse.org

Provides emotional support and advocacy for spouses and children of the chronically ill or disabled.

Books and Publications

Babcock, Elise N. *When Life Becomes Precious: A Guide for Loved Ones and Friends of Cancer Patients.* New York: Bantam Books, 1997.

Berman, Claire. *Caring for Yourself While Caring for Your Aging Parents.* New York: Henry Holt and Company, 1996.

Capossela, C., and S. Warnock. *Share the Care: How to Organize a Group to Care for Someone Who Is Seriously Ill.* New York: Fireside, 1995.

Carter, Rosalynn, with Susan Golant. *Helping Yourself Help Others: A Book for Caregivers.* New York: Random House, 1994.

Gray-Davidson, Frena. *The Alzheimer's Sourcebook for Caregivers: A Practical Guide for Getting through the Day.* Los Angeles: Lowell House, 1999.

Johnson, Veronica. *At the Crossroads: The Insider Guide to Nursing Home Placement and Caring for the Needs of the Elderly.* Veronica Birdsong Publishers, 2000.

McFarlane, Rodger, and Philip Bashe. *The Complete Bedside Companion: No-Nonsense Advice to Caring for the Seriously Ill.* New York: Simon and Schuster, 1998.

Miller, James E. *When You're Ill or Incapacitated/When You're the Caregiver.* Fort Wayne, Ind.: Willowgreen Publishing, 1995.

Miller, James E. *The Caregiver's Book: Caring for Another, Caring for Yourself.* Minneapolis: Augsburg Fortress, 1996.

Samples, Pat. *Daily Comforts for Caregivers.* Minneapolis: Fairview Press, 1999.

Wilkinson, James A. *A Family Caregiver's Guide to Planning and Decision Making for the Elderly.* Minneapolis: Fairview Press, 1999.

Home Care and In-Home Services

Agencies, Organizations, and Web Sites

Meals-on-Wheels Association of America

1414 Prince Street, Suite 302

Alexandria, VA 22314

800-677-1116

703-548-5558

Web site: www.projectmeal.org

Provides information about the Meals-on-Wheels program in your area.

National Association for Home Care (NAHC)

228 Seventh Street S.E.

Washington, DC 20003

202-547-7424

Web site: www.nahc.org

NAHC is the nation's largest trade association representing the interests and concerns of home care agencies, hospices, home care aide organizations, and medical equipment suppliers. Provides consumers with helpful information about home care and how to choose a home care service.

Books and Publications

Friedman, Jo-Ann. *Home Healthcare: A Complete Guide for Patients and Their Families.* New York: W. W. Norton and Company, 1986.

Wilkinson, James A. *A Family Caregiver's Guide to Planning and Decision Making for the Elderly.* Minneapolis: Fairview Press, 1999.

Hospice and End-of-Life Care

Agencies, Organizations, and Web Sites

American Hospice Foundation
2120 L Street N.W., Suite 200
Washington, DC 20037
202-223-0204
Web site: www.americanhospice.org
E-mail: ahf@msn.com

Advances the hospice concept of care and promotes hospices that seek to meet growing and complex needs. By forging new partnerships at the local and national levels, the foundation ensures the availability of hospice care for many people who might otherwise fall through the cracks. Offers articles, publications, and workshops about death, dying, grief, and bereavement.

Americans for Better Care of the Dying (ABCD)

4125 Albemarle Street N.W., Suite 210

Washington, DC 20016

202-895-9485

202-895-9486

Web site: www.abcd-caring.org

E-mail: info@abcd-caring.org

Dedicated to ensuring that all Americans can count on good end-of-life care, ABCD focuses its efforts on improved pain management, financial reimbursement systems, continuity of care, support for family caregivers, public policy, and other fundamental reforms.

Dying Well

Web site: www.dyingwell.org

Provides referrals to various organizations, links to related Web sites, and publications that empower people with life-threatening illness and their families.

Growth House, Inc.

415-255-9045

Web site: www.growthhouse.org

E-mail: info@growthhouse.org

Provides comprehensive resources about life-threatening and terminal illnesses, hospice and home care, pain management, palliative care, death, and bereavement.

Hospice Foundation of America
2001 S Street N.W., #300
Washington, DC 20009
800-854-3402
Fax: 202-638-5312
Web site: www.hospicefoundation.org

Hospice Foundation of America is a not-for-profit organization that provides leadership in the development and application of hospice care. Through professional development, research, public education, and information, Hospice Foundation of America assists those who cope personally or professionally with terminal illness, death, and grief. Provides access to videotapes and publications about end-of-life care and grief.

Last Acts Campaign
1035 30th Street N.W.
Washington, DC 20007
202-338-9790
Web site: www.lastacts.org

Provides information on end-of-life care and new legislation. Also offers on-line discussion groups and many helpful links to related sites.

The National Hospice and Palliative Care Organization (NHPCO)
1700 Diagonal Road, Suite 300
Alexandria, VA 22314
703-837-1500
Web site: www.nhpco.org
E-mail: info@nhpco.org

NHPCO is a professional organization that also provides information to consumers about hospice care and services nationwide.

National Hospice Foundation
P.O. Box 993
Falls Church, VA 22040-9851
800-658-8898

Provides information on hospice programs available in your area, as well as general information about hospice services.

On Our Own Terms—Moyers on Dying Web Site:
www.pbs.org/wnet/onourownterms/index.html

Provides information about decision making and end-of-life care. Based on the Bill Moyers series, "On Our Own Terms."

Books and Publications

All about Hospice: A Consumer's Guide. Washington, DC: Foundation for Hospice and Homecare, 1991. (To order a free copy, call 202-546-4759, or visit the Web site www.hospice-america.org.)

Bolen, Jean S. *Close to the Bone: Life-Threatening Illness and the Search for Meaning.* New York: Scribner, 1996.

Byock, Ira. *Dying Well: The Prospect for Growth at the End of Life.* New York: Riverhead Books, 1997.

Choosing Hospice: A Consumer's Guide. St. Paul: Minnesota Hospice Organization, 1997. (Call MHO at 651-659-0423 to order a free copy.)

Doka, Kenneth J. *Living with Life-Threatening Illness: A Guide for Patients, Their Families and Caregivers.* Lanham, Md.: Lexington Books, 1993.

Doka, Kenneth J., and Joyce Davidson, eds. *Living with Grief: When Illness Is Prolonged*. Bristol, Pa.: Taylor and Francis, 1997.

Dunn, Hank. *Hard Choices for Loving People: CPR, Artificial Feeding, Comfort Measures Only and the Elderly Patient*. Herndon, Va.: A and A Publishers, 1994.

Fairview Health Services. *A Family Handbook of Hospice Care*. Minneapolis: Fairview Press, 1999.

Kübler-Ross, Elisabeth. *To Live until We Say Goodbye*. Upper Saddle River, N.J.: Prentice-Hall, 1978.

Lattanzi-Licht, Marcia, with Jay Mahoney. *The Hospice Choice: In Pursuit of a Peaceful Death*. New York: Simon and Schuster, 1998.

Lynn, Joanne, and Joan Harrold. *Handbook for Mortals: Guidance for People Facing Serious Illness*. New York: Oxford University Press, 1999.

Pelaez, Martha, and Paul Rothman. *A Guide for Recalling and Telling Your Life Story*. Washington, D.C.: Hospice Foundation of America, 1994. (To order, call 800-854-3402.)

Sankar, Andrea. *Dying at Home: A Family Guide for Caregiving*. Baltimore: Johns Hopkins University Press, 1991.

Tobin, Daniel R., with Karen Lindsay. *Peaceful Dying: The Step-by-Step Guide to Preserving Your Dignity, Your Choices, and Your Inner Peace at the End of Life*. Reading, Mass.: Perseus Books, 1999.

Legal, Financial, and Insurance Issues

Agencies, Organizations, and Web Sites

AARP Legal Services Network

601 E Street N.W.
Washington, DC 20049
800-424-3410
Web site: www.aarp.org

AARP members are entitled to a free half-hour consultation with a lawyer from the AARP Legal Services Network.

American Bar Association Commission on the Legal Problems of the Elderly

740 15th Street N.W.
Washington, DC 20005-1022
202-662-8690
Web site: www.abanet.org/elderly
E-mail: abaelderly@abanet.org

The ABA Commission on Legal Problems of the Elderly (CLPE) is dedicated to examining the law-related concerns of older persons. Established by the American Bar Association in 1978, the commission has sought to improve legal services for the elderly, particularly through involvement of the private bar, and has explored legal issues surrounding long-term care, surrogate decision making, elder abuse, individual rights, guardianship, housing, social security, and other public benefit programs.

The Estate Planning Web Site

Web site: www.estateplanninglinks.com

Internet directory providing hundreds of links to estate planning, elderlaw, and tax-related Web sites for consumers and professionals.

Judge David L. Bazelon Center for Mental Health Law

1101 15th Street N.W., Suite 1212
Washington, DC 20005-5002
202-467-5730

Provides nationwide legal support for elderly people who have mental disabilities.

Medicare Hotline

800-638-6833

A general number to call if you have questions about Medicare.

National Insurance Consumer Helpline

800-942-4242

Offers consumer information about auto, business, home owner's, life, disaster, and other types of insurance.

U.S. Department of Health and Human Services

Social Security Administration
7500 Security Boulevard
Baltimore, MD 21244-1850
800-772-1213
Web site: www.ssa.gov

Contact for questions about social security benefits.

Books and Publications

Wilkinson, James A. *A Family Caregiver's Guide to Planning and Decision Making for the Elderly*. Minneapolis: Fairview Press, 1999.

Disease

Agencies, Organizations, and Web sites

Alzheimer's Association
919 North Michigan Avenue, Suite 1100
Chicago, IL 60611-1676
800-272-3900
312-335-8700
Web site: www.alz.org

ALS Association
27001 Agoura Road, Suite 150
Calabasas Hills, CA 91301-5104
800-782-4747
Web site: www.alsa.org

American Cancer Society (ACS)
1599 Clifton Road N.E.
Atlanta, GA 30329-4251
800-ACS-2345 (800-227-2345)
Web site: www.cancer.org

Connects people with local ACS offices, which provide information about cancer, treatment, financial assistance, and support resources. Local offices may pay for medical equipment and supplies.

American Diabetes Association

1701 North Beauregard Street

Alexandria, VA 22311

1-800-DIABETES (342-2383)

Web site: www.diabetes.org

American Heart Association

7272 Greenville Avenue

Dallas, TX 75231

800-242-8721

214-373-6300

Web site: www.americanheart.org

American Lung Association

1740 Broadway

New York, NY 10019-4374

800-586-4872

212-315-8700

Web site: www.lungusa.org

Mental Health Information Center

800-969-NMHA (6642)

TTY: 800-433-5959

Web site: www.nmha.org

National AIDS Hotline

800-342-2437

Web site: www.cdc.gov/hiv/hivinfo/nah.htm

Operated by the Centers for Disease Control and Prevention, this twenty-four-hour hotline provides information about HIV and AIDS. Referral services and publications are also offered.

National Cancer Institute
Cancer Information Center
31 Center Drive, Room 10A-03
MSC 2580
Bethesda, MD 20893
800-422-6237
301-402-5874
Web site: www.icic.nci.nih.gov

National Institute of Diabetes and Digestive and Kidney Diseases
Information Office
31 Center Drive, Room 9A-04
MSC 2560
Bethesda, MD 20892-3560
301-496-3583

National Institute of Neurological Disorders and Stroke (NINDS)
Information Office
31 Center Drive, Room 8A-06
MSC 2540
Bethesda, MD 20892-2540
800-352-9424
301-496-5751

National Mental Health Association
1021 Prince Street
Alexandria, VA 22314-2971
703-684-7722
Fax: 703-684-5968

Stroke Network

Web site: www.strokenetwork.com

On-line support and information for stroke survivors and caregivers.

Books and Publications

Adam, Francis V. *The Breathing Disorders Sourcebook.* Los Angeles: Lowell House, 1998.

Fairview Health Services. *Living Well with Heart Disease.* Minneapolis: Fairview Press, 2000.

Gehling, Eve. *The Family and Friends' Guide to Diabetes: Everything You Need to Know.* New York: John Wiley and Sons, 2000.

Gersh, Bernard J., and Michael B. Wood. *Mayo Clinic Heart Book.* New York: William Morrow and Co., 2000.

Gray-Davidson, Frena. *The Alzheimer's Sourcebook for Caregivers: A Practical Guide for Getting through the Day.* Los Angeles: Lowell House, 1999.

Larkin, Marilynn. *When Someone You Love Has a Stroke.* New York: Dell Publishing, 1995.

Noller, Gail A. *Finding Your Way: Families and the Cancer Survivor.* Minneapolis: American Cancer Society, 1998. (To order your free copy, call the ACS at 800-582-5152 or 612-925-2772.)

Funeral Planning

Agencies, Organizations, and Web Sites

American Association of Retired Persons (AARP)

601 E Street N.W.

Washington, DC 20049

800-424-3410

Web site: www.aarp.org

Provides information on wills, living trusts, funerals, and burials.

Funeral Consumers Alliance

P.O. Box 10

Heinsburg, VT 05461

800-458-5563

Web site: www.funerals.org/famsa

Provides information on low-cost funeral planning.

Funeral Service Educational Foundation

National Funeral Directors Association

13625 Bishops Drive

Brookfield, WI 53005

800-228-6332

262-789-1880

Web site: www.nfda.org

The Funeral Service Educational Foundation offers a wide variety of books, videos, and audiotapes on topics ranging from children and grief to public health.

GLOSSARY

Advance care planning: A thoughtful family discussion about wishes and goals for end-of-life care. The goals of advance care planning include 1) determining the care a person would want if faced with a life-threatening or life-limiting illness, 2) naming one or more healthcare agents, and 3) completing a written healthcare directive.

Advance directive: A legal document in which people can 1) state their wishes regarding medical treatment in the event that they are incapacitated, and 2) name one or more healthcare agents who will make decisions for them if they cannot speak for themselves. Advance directives are sometimes called "living wills" or "healthcare directives."

Agent: See Healthcare agent.

Artificial nutrition and hydration: A variety of therapies that prevent malnutrition or dehydration in patients who cannot swallow. Artificial nutrition and hydration may include intravenous (IV) therapy, total parenteral nutrition (TPN), nasogastric tube (NG tube) feedings, and gastric tube (G tube) feedings.

Comfort care: Care that relieves pain and suffering and controls debilitating symptoms but does not prevent death. Comfort care can include medications as well as nonpharmaceutical treatments for pain, anxiety, constipation, breathing difficulties, and other symptoms; personal care such as bathing and turning; emotional and spiritual support; and other treatments that enhance comfort.

CPR (cardiopulmonary resuscitation): A group of treatments used when a person's heart or breathing stops. CPR can include mouth-to-mouth breathing, chest compressions, electric shock, and heart-stimulating drugs.

Decision-making capacity: The ability to understand significant benefits, risks, and alternatives to proposed treatments, and to make and communicate healthcare decisions.

Dialysis: Treatment that replaces the function of the kidneys. With hemodialysis, which is done for several hours three times per week, the patient is hooked up to a machine that cleans the blood and then returns the blood to the body. With peritoneal dialysis, which is done at home several times per day, a special solution is injected into a tube that is stitched into the lower abdomen. This solution absorbs bodily wastes (which would normally be removed by the kidneys) and is then drained from the body.

DNI (Do Not Intubate) order: A medical order, written and signed by a physician, not to pass a tube into a patient's windpipe to facilitate breathing.

DNR (Do Not Resuscitate) order: A medical order, written and signed by a physician, not to apply CPR in order to restore normal breathing or restart a failed heartbeat. Also called "no code."

Ethical will: A written document containing experiences, ideas, and thoughts that an individual wishes to pass on to loved ones. Ethical wills come from an old Jewish tradition of leaving a legacy of values to the next generation.

Feeding tube: See NG (nasogastric) tube or G (gastric) tube.

Futile measures: A general term used to characterize interventions that are expected to have little effect on the outcome or prognosis of a seriously ill or terminal patient.

G (gastric) tube: A tube that is surgically inserted into a patient's stomach, allowing for the administration of liquid nutrition.

Healthcare agent: The person designated in an advance directive to make decisions for a patient if ever the patient loses decision-making capacity. In most cases, the healthcare agent is a family member. Also called "healthcare proxy" or "medical power of attorney."

Healthcare directive: See Advance directive.

Hemodialysis: See Dialysis.

Hospice: A philosophy of care for dying patients that emphasizes comfort over cure. It includes physical, emotional, and spiritual support for the patient and family; pain and symptom management; and grief support services. Most hospice care occurs in the home, but it may also be given in hospitals, nursing homes, and other facilities. To enroll in hospice, the patient must 1) have a terminal prognosis of six months or less (as certified by a physician), and 2) agree to pursue comfort care instead of curative or life-prolonging treatment.

Hospice Medicare benefit: A special benefit under Medicare that covers hospice services. The benefit includes the cost for nurses, social workers, chaplains, home health aides, and therapists; coverage for all prescriptions and treatments related to the terminal illness; in-patient respite care; medical equipment, such as oxygen or a hospital bed; on-call, twenty-four-hour hospice service; and bereavement follow-up for the family.

Intubation: Placing a breathing tube down or into a patient's trachea (windpipe) so the patient can be hooked up to a ventilator (artificial breathing machine).

IV (intravenous) therapy: Fluids and medications placed directly into the patient's bloodstream through a vein.

Life-supporting treatment: Treatments that replace or support a bodily function that is failing.

Living will: See Advance directive.

Medical power of attorney: See Healthcare agent.

NG (nasogastric) tube: A tube placed through a patient's nose, down the esophagus, and into the stomach, allowing for the administration of liquid nutrition.

Palliative care: Treatment and care focused on relieving symptoms and providing comfort. Palliative care addresses the physical, emotional, and spiritual needs of a patient and family and can be provided throughout all stages of an illness.

Peritoneal dialysis: See Dialysis.

Physician-assisted suicide (PAS): Upon the request of a terminally ill patient, a physician provides the means to hasten death.

Currently, Oregon is the only state that allows PAS, and only under strict protocols.

Respirator: See Ventilator.

Terminal illness: An incurable and irreversible illness or condition. When a person is diagnosed as terminally ill, death is expected within a relatively short period of time.

TPN (total parenteral nutrition): Nutrients placed directly into the patient's bloodstream via a special catheter inserted into a large vein.

Ventilator: A machine that helps a patient breathe. Ventilators can be used temporarily until a person can breathe without assistance, or as a permanent breathing aid. Also called a "vent," "respirator," or "breathing machine."

INDEX

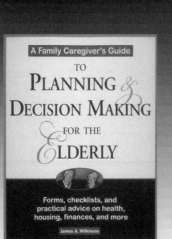